*A Pictorial Journey to Japan's Cultural Treasures*

# The BEAUTY of JAPAN

Gakken

# The BEAUTY of JAPAN

## A Pictorial Journey to Japan's Cultural Treasures

Editorial Consultant
    Nakayama Kaneyoshi (Associate Professor of English, Tokoha Gakuen Fuji Junior College)
Translator
    Sekimori Gaynor (LOGOSTIKS)
English Language Advisor
    William Feuillan (The Japan Times)
Book Design
    Shimada Takushi
Illustrations
    Shiba Yuji
Map
    Kimura Zugeisha


Editorial Staff
    Anzai Tatsuo (Managing Editor)
    Kisu Production
Publishing Manager (Planning)
    Tachibana Yukio

Foreword by Edward Seidensticker (Professor Emeritus of Japanese, Columbia University)
Jacket Photo: The five-storied pagoda of Kofukuji (Nara)
Jacket (Back): Overgarment with a design of running water, cherry blossoms, wisteria, yamabuki,
              mandarin ducks. (Rakuto Museum, Kyoto)
Title page:    Arashiyama (Kyoto)
Pages 2 & 3:  The Mount Wakakusa Fire Festival (Nara)

# THE BEAUTY OF JAPAN

Copyright © 1990 by GAKKEN Co., Ltd.
All rights reserved, including the right to reproduce this book or portions
thereof in any form without the written permission of the publisher.

Published by GAKKEN Co., Ltd.
4-40-5 Kami-ikedai, Ohta-ku, Tokyo 145, Japan

Overseas distributors: Japan Publications Trading Co., Ltd.
P.O. Box 5030 Tokyo International, Tokyo 100-31, Japan

**Distributors:**
UNITED STATES: Kodansha America Inc., through Farrar, Straus & Giroux,
19 Union Square West, New York, NY 10003.
CANADA: Fitzhenry & Whiteside Ltd., 195 Allstate Parkway, Markham, Ontario L3R 4T8.
BRITISH ISLES AND EUROPEAN CONTINENT: Premier Book Marketing Ltd.,
1 Gower Street, London WC1E 6HA.
AUSTRALIA AND NEW ZEALAND: Bookwise International, 54 Crittenden Road, Findon,
South Australia 5023.
THE FAR EAST AND JAPAN: Japan Publications Trading Co., Ltd., 1-2-1, Sarugaku-cho,
Chiyoda-ku, Tokyo 101, Japan.

First edition 1991
ISBN: 0-87040-862-3
ISBN: 4-05-151300-9 (in Japan)
Printed in Japan

# CONTENTS

# FOREWORD

Edward Seidensticker

**Edward Seidensticker,** well-known scholar of Japanese culture and Professor Emeritus of Japanese, Columbia University.

The Japanese are right to complain that the world does not pay enough attention to them. The fact that almost every people could make the same complaint with similar justification does not alter its validity. Japan does not get the attention which a powerful nation deserves. There are exceptions, peoples that pay adequate attention. Koreans are very much aware of Japan. But Europeans and Americans, whom the Japanese have chiefly in mind when they use the expression *gaijin*, "outsider" or "alien," are not, except as a commercial and mercantile threat. The notions prevalent about Japan in most of the world and perhaps all of the *gaijin* part tend to be half-truths.

For those interested in aesthetics and the arts, the notion of austerity and restraint and studied rusticity has prevailed. Some years ago—I am not sure whether it is still true or not—the Japanese word *shibui* had currency in the world of high fashion in such places as New York. *Shibui*, which is an adjective, though it was most commonly used in New York as a noun, was held to be the essence of Japanese taste. It has among the standard dictionary definitions "astringent" and "sober." So, by a remarkable coincidence, does "austere." Complex words in two languages do not often cover the same range of meanings; but these two do.

We may reasonably conclude that the realm of severe, withdrawn taste covered by *shibui* is not exclusively Japanese. It is held all the same to be characteristically Japanese, as its English counterpart, the austere, is not held to be characteristically European or American. It is also held to be a uniquely Japanese contribution to the aesthetics of the world. *Shibui* is not the only Japanese word applied to withdrawn, subdued beauty, but the sum of them comes to an emphasis on plainness and understatement that is held to be peculiarly Japanese.

Plainness the world over can lead to an appearance of rusticity. We have the example of the Shakers and their imitators in the United States. It may in its origins be rustic. A Japanese wandering past a Korean well sees a kitchen vessel that seems to him, with an eye accustomed to looking for beauty in a clod of earth, very beautiful. So he takes it back across the straits and shows it to his fellow literati, and over the centuries it becomes an object beyond pricing. The appearance of rusticity may on the other hand be highly contrived.

The cult of the severe, restrained, and rustic has seldom dominated Japanese aesthetics completely. Since the Middle Ages, which expression we may take to mean roughly the centuries between 1200 and 1600, it has always been present in some measure. Before then it was scarcely present at all as a conscious and articulated principle. It is essentially a product of the Middle Ages.

Many will give credit for its emergence to Zen Buddhism. Others will give the larger share of credit to *chanoyu.* This is the highly formalized making and taking of tea that is often, though not ideally, called "tea ceremony" in English. Zen and *chanoyu* are not easily separated. The intellectual and emotional tendencies of early tea masters were strongly Zen. Yet it was in *chanoyu* that the aesthetics of restraint emerged most explicitly. The reader of these pages will come upon the *chashitsu,* the room or cottage in which the "ceremony" is held. The designs are sometimes bold but always simple, and the builders have never lost awareness of the rustic dwellings that were the original inspiration. It was in this setting that Korean kitchen bowls, along with such unpretentious artifacts as whisks and scoops, were admired into pricelessness.

The aesthetics of restraint did not disappear with the end of the Middle Ages and the coming of the Tokugawa shoguns, whose advent is held by many to mark the advent of modern times, and certainly meant the beginning of a very different sort of cultural epoch. Yet some of the great masterpieces of medieval aesthetics, highly sophisticated dwellings still retaining an appearance of the rustic, for instance, are from the Tokugawa Period. A superior example is the Katsura Detached Palace in Kyoto, photographs of which will be found in these pages. It is not a single building but a complex, a harmonious composition of buildings and grounds. Nothing about it shouts for attention, and yet the subdued tones and the unassertive proportions are immediately pleasing to the eye. Some viewers may see for themselves but most have to have pointed out the extreme care and skill that have gone into the fabrication of the least obtrusive line and the smallest fitting.

One no longer sees in the Japanese countryside many of the

farm cottages that inspired this sort of architecture. Modern convenience has done away with most of them and is rapidly doing away with the rest, except for the few that have been sorted out for government protection. It is a sad but undeniable fact that, though the Japanese countryside is still rich in natural beauty, the man-made objects are not as beautiful as they used to be. The pinks and blues of mass-produced tiles prevail over the neutral tones of earlier materials, such as thatch. It is rare even in the big and hugely wealthy cities to come upon a new building with a pure traditional exterior. Interiors, on the other hand, may still have the dusky simplicity praised by the novelist Tanizaki in his beautiful essay on shadows. This is most likely to be true of restaurants specializing in the Japanese cuisine. They are quite possibly the most expensive restaurants in the world, but this does not make them too expensive if one thinks of the meal as an experience in beauty and the surroundings as another.

The aesthetics of restraint might not have seemed to the world so dominant in the Japanese arts if the Japanese had been in control of the matter. Foreigners probably had more to do with it than Japanese. Insecure in what beliefs they had, the Japanese were happy enough to go along when something of theirs was praised. Praise fell most generously on buildings like those of the Katsura Detached Palace and their equivalent in the other arts. Though there had been a flurry of japonaiserie in the nineteenth century, the German architect Bruno Taut, who came to Japan in 1933, was the most prominent of early twentieth-century evangelists. He had numerous followers, especially in the United States, during the years after the Second World War when Zen was much in vogue. So strong was Taut's influence that one was reluctant to admit to a feeling that more exuberant and daring flights in architecture and the other arts also had something to recommend them. To admit it was to admit one's own bad taste. Of recent years the balance has been restored.

For to dwell exclusively on austere creations is to be guilty of half-truth. Not all half-truths are harmful. Since it is so far from disseminating bad taste, this one cannot be called so. Yet a half-truth it remains. The highly colored thing may indeed be the really Japanese thing. It can be argued that color is what the Japanese are really good at. The monochrome thing, perhaps, the Chinese do better. Fanciers of calligraphy may conclude, reluctantly, that the Chinese sense of line is the stronger and steadier. At color the Japanese are unsurpassed. It is often a bold use of color, putting side by side two colors that are in much danger of clashing, and it sometimes seems almost voracious, trying to overflow the borders of a painting. Not all premedieval works of art are highly colored, and some leave unpainted spaces in ample measure, as upholders of the highly Chinese medieval view say that all Japanese paintings should do. The great masterpiece of Heian courtly art, the scrolls illustrating *The Tale of Genji*, does nothing of the sort. It is by more than one artist, and the artists do not show identical tastes in their use of color. This artist is bolder and more abandoned than that one. Yet the work as a whole is highly colored, and no space is left unfilled. Probably it was considerably gayer when it was first painted, in the twelfth century, than it is now. Parts of it have deteriorated badly.

*Genji monogatari emaki* (**Picture Scroll of scenes from "*The Tale of Genji*."**) **"Takekawa" 2. Tokugawa Art Museum, Nagoya, National Treasure** It is spring. On the left, two court ladies are absorbed in a game of *go*, while their attendants are enjoying the cherry blossom, seated on the *engawa*. To the right, a nobleman is peeping in from the outside. The scroll dates from the early twelfth century, and is based upon the eleventh century novel by Murasaki Shikibu, "*The Tale of Genji*."

**The Kusotei. Exterior (left), interior (right)** A tea room designed by Oda Urakusai (1547–1621), a feudal lord and a tea master, who was a younger brother of Oda Nobunaga, the first of the great unifiers of the sixteenth century. While continuing the orthodox tea style systematized by Sen no Rikyu (1522–1591), Urakusai brought to it a new freshness. The Kusotei (literally "nine windows," after the nine windows of its structure) is an Important Cultural Property. It is said to have been constructed initially in the grounds of Azuchi Castle in Shiga Prefecture; it is now preserved in the Sankeien Garden in Yokohama.

In a sense it is restrained. It is not realistic. The artists decline to express openly the intense emotions that are depicted. Nowhere, however, is there a suggestion that free and generous use of color need be considered in any way vulgar. The aesthetics of restraint had their great day in the Middle Ages, and in the sixteenth century the old delight in color emerged once more, enlivened and invigorated, it almost seemed, by having lain somewhat dormant—it never was completely dormant—for so long. The first Japanese art form to attract considerable interest among the people who matter most, artists, was the ukiyoe polychrome woodcut. This is rather like the *Genji* scrolls, abstract and stylized in the depiction of the human form and human feelings, free in the use of color.

There are many other specimens of Japanese beauty in these pages that accord very badly with the notion that restraint is everything. One became aware when the Kinkaku (Golden Pavilion) in Kyoto was destroyed by an arsonist in 1950 and then rebuilt that time had been a deceiver, contributing greatly to the half-truth about sober restraint as the most Japanese of aesthetic principles. Much of the gold leaf with which the

building had been covered had peeled away, and soft, ligneous tones prevailed. It was rebuilt, and all the dazzle which must have been there originally was there again. This was a medieval building which most certainly did not hide its light. What restraint seemed to be evident in the old building had been imposed by the centuries.

A pre-medieval building from which the dazzle has never been allowed to disappear is also in these pages: the Konjikido (Golden Hall) of the Chusonji in northern Japan. A smaller religious edifice than the Kinkaku, the Konjikido too was covered with gold leaf, and from the Middle Ages a larger building was put up over and all around it to shelter it from the elements. So the original gold is still in place. Neither building is to be described as garish, and neither is in the smallest measure restrained. The Japanese too love color and glitter, and are very good at them.

But the buildings that suffered most from the notion that the best of Japanese art is restrained were probably the mortuary shrines of the first and third Tokugawa shoguns at Nikko, north of Tokyo. Looking at the brilliant decoration in the somberness of cryptomeria groves and thinking the combination very fine indeed, one wondered that one could have such poor taste as to like them. Of recent decades it has become possible once more to like them unapologetically.

So in these pages we have the whole truth, the half-truth complemented by the other half. The beautiful things of Japan are sometimes restrained and sometimes exuberant and almost baroque. There are bound to be failures along the way, the austere becoming merely dreary, the exuberant becoming garish; but when either predilection leads to success it leads to supreme success.

Sometimes the two are to be found in intimate association. A few afternoons at the theater can establish this fascinating and puzzling fact. There should be several afternoons, because the form to be recommended is Noh, and Noh takes getting used to. It is the stateliest and most ritualized of forms, so slow that watching it makes the muscles ache, changing little over the centuries, offering very little room for individual expression; and laid over all the restraint and stylization is a coat of many colors, the costuming. They did not always go together, but they do now, and the juxtaposition jars no one.

**Red Raku tea bowl**   Height 8 cm., circumference 11.5 cm. A tea bowl that was a favorite of the great tea master, Sen no Rikyu. At first, tea bowls used in the tea ceremony were regular works of Chinese make; gradually though practitioners came to prefer the rougher style that originated on the Korean peninsula, and it was on this that bowls pleasing to the Japanese aesthetic were based.

# IN SEARCH OF
# AN ETERNAL BEAUTY

# Nature in a Large-scale Decorative Painting

What draws our attention when we go around looking at old temples and warriors' residences in Japan is how much a room is surrounded by paintings—on walls, sliding doors, and on the screens used as room partitions. The majority of these paintings feature natural designs of plants and flowers. Even indoors, the nature-loving Japanese wanted to enjoy the feeling of being surrounded by natural beauty.

Temples and the mansions of the nobility had employed such decoration from very early on, but the trend became widely diffused from around the sixteenth century. In the course of that century, the incessant fighting of the past hundred years began to give way to a more settled society through the reunification efforts of generals such as Oda Nobunaga (1534–82), Toyotomi Hideyoshi (1536–98) and Tokugawa Ieyasu (1542–1616). As their position strengthened, they had huge mansions and castles built and decorated them in a grandiose style, to the wonder of all who saw them. The paintings that ornamented the new buildings demanded imposing composition and strong brushwork.

As peace returned to the country, this tradition took root in the *chonin* (The townsmen of urban administrative district) culture that then began to flourish, and by the time of the resplendent Genroku era (1688–1704) it had become beloved of a broad spectrum of people.

**(Above left) Pair of two-panel folding screens, "Red and White Plum Trees" (*Kohakubai zu*) by Ogata Korin (1658–1716)** MOA Museum of Art, Atami, Shizuoka Prefecture. Red and white plum blossoms flower on a background of gold leaf, and are separated by a river drawn in silver leaf. The blue whirlpool pattern depicting the current of the water is painted smoothly but boldly. The painting's vitality comes from various contrasting elements in the large-scale composition—the white and the red plum blossoms, the straight lines of the sharp branches and the gentle curving lines of the river, and the realistic depiction of the flowers against the abstract way the flow of the water has been shown. This screen is one of the greatest achievements of the Japanese aesthetic tradition.

Ogata Korin worked as a textile and decorative art designer at the same time as studying painting. Though he suffered many setbacks, economic and spiritual, he established a distinct Japanese style of decorative painting.

**(Above) Detail from *Maples*, painting on sliding-door panels (*fusuma*) by Hasegawa Tohaku (1539–1610), Chishakuin, Kyoto**
Branches of the bending and twisting maples powerfully traverse the painting. The gold-leaf background and the brightly colored grasses and flowers entwining themselves in disordered profusion around the maple give the work a vivid freshness.

The painting originally was one of a series that decorated the sliding doors of a temple called Shounji, built by Hideyoshi for the soul of his dead infant child, Sutematsu. Shounji, which when completed was con-sidered the most splendid of all the temples of Kyoto, was destroyed by fire, and only the door panels escaped destruction. Most of them were placed in the care of the present Chishakuin.

Hasegawa Tohaku was noted primarily for his ink painting (*suiboku*), but here he exhibits his great skill in polychrome and gilt works. The genius who depicted nature in his ink paintings was able to transfer his talents to the demands of a new age.

# The Delights of Nature in Art

The Japanese like looking at flowers and plants outdoors. Cherry blossom-viewing and admiring maple leaves are two traditional events which have survived to the present day. Certain places are known for their displays of cherry blossoms and maple leaves, and during the cherry blossom-viewing season in particular, around the beginning of April, people join their colleagues to drink together and sing under the cherry trees. In Japan, to say "flower-viewing" is really to mean looking at the cherry blossoms.

Such events centering on the delights of nature have long been a theme for paintings. Though from century to century the customs and manners of the people depicted might differ, the happy revelers themselves never change.

**(Above) Cherry blossom-viewing**
Modern people might seem to delight in the beauty of the cherry blossom for its own sake, but underlying their simple enjoyment are the varied emotions of the Japanese of old.

**(Left) Screen depicting scenes from everyday life, Detail, Tokyo National Museum, Painted ca. 16th century, Aristocrats and warriors looking at cherry blossoms**
Flower viewing originated from an ancient agricultural ritual that predicted the extent of the rice harvest by the way the cherry trees bloomed. From around the tenth century, this ritual became a pastime for the nobility. Cherry blossoms bloom suddenly and fall only a few days later. Aristocrats would write many poems on the theme, for the cherry symbolized for them the transience of life, how short was earthly splendor. With the emergence of the warriors as dominant figures in Japanese society, cherry blossoms took on another nuance—they reminded the samurai of what was brave and upright, of the ability to die a manly death in case of need, and not cling to life.

**(Above) Detail from *Maple-Viewing at Takao*, screen painting (*byobu-e*) by Kano Hideyori (fl. ca. 1564–77), Tokyo National Museum** Mount Takao, north of Kyoto, has long been a place noted for the beauty of its autumn maples, and today continues to attract crowds of visitors during the maple-viewing season. The screen depicts a wide range of people from all classes delighting in their own ways in the colorful leaves; shown here is the famous detail depicting women drinking and partying under the trees, loose-sashed and sprawling, suggesting to us the robustness of sixteenth century plebeian life.

# Mount Fuji in Woodblock Prints

Mount Fuji, at 3,776 meters, is Japan's tallest mountain. Its distinctive shape has made it the subject of poetry from ancient times, as well as the object of a religious cult.

Mount Fuji is not one peak among many in a mountain range, but a free-standing conically-shaped stratovolcano formed by the accumulation of volcanic debris. Because it is free-standing, it dominates its surroundings, and its beautiful shape is visible from a great distance. It is rare for stratovolcanos to rise more than a thousand meters; Mount Fuji's great height can be attributed to the fact that it was formed in three stages—the original mountain of hundreds of thousands of years ago, the volcanic proto-Fuji, and the additional layers of the modern mountain.

The graceful mountain has been beloved of generations of artists. Here we will examine how it was portrayed in the scenic woodblock prints that reached their height of popularity in the nineteenth century.

Woodblock prints (*ukiyoe*) flourished in the eighteenth and nineteenth centuries. Literally "pictures of the floating world," they tended to deal with the pleasures of human society, and took as their themes acclaimed beauties, actors and the life of the common people. By the nineteenth century, a separate genre had emerged dealing with the beauties of nature, for which Katsushika Hokusai (1760–1849) and Utagawa (Ando) Hiroshige (1797–1858) are the most well-known artists.

**(Above) Mount Fuji, a modern sacred peak** Because of its dominating yet beautiful form, Mount Fuji has since ancient times been the object of a popular religious cult as well as a place where practitioners of mountain religion carry out their rites. Popular faith in the mountain accelerated from around the beginning of the eighteenth century. Specialized guides and practitioners called *oshi* who took pilgrims up the mountain and ran special lodgings for them made their appearance, and particularly in Edo (Tokyo), tens of thousands of people joined pilgrim organizations. Even today, a cult still exists which considers Mount Fuji itself to be a god, and when the mountain is officially opened to climbers on July 1, white-clad ascetics perform rituals and climb to the summit before the general public can proceed.

**(Below)** *Hakone, Hara, Yui,* **woodblock prints from the series "Fifty-three Stages of the Tokaido" by Hiroshige, 1833, Tokyo National Museum**

In 1832, Hiroshige traveled for the first time along the Tokaido, the trunk route between Edo and Kyoto, in the retinue of a government official delivering a horse to the imperial court. The sketches he made then and the impressions he received from this journey inspired him to produce the following year the famous Tokaido series. The sharpness of his perception is apparent in the distant views of Mount Fuji, in which he skillfully combines near and distant perspective. His restrained and serene style, in deep contrast to Hokusai's unique lines and coloration, was deeply loved for its tranquility and lyricism. It was through the influence of Hiroshige that landscape prints became diffused among the common people.

(Above) *Kanagawaoki namiura* (Beneath the Waves off Kanagawa)
(Left) *Gaifu kaisei* (Wind in Clear Weather, "Red Fuji")
Woodblock prints from the series *Fugaku sanjurokkei* (The Thirty-six Views of Mount Fuji) by Katsushika Hokusai, Ca. 1831, Tokyo National Museum

Though Hokusai had a remarkable talent for depicting the manners and customs of his time, his true genius was in his unique landscape prints, in which he incorporated the European law of perspective into the *ukiyoe* form. "The Thirty-six Views of Mount Fuji" was the first instance in which the theme of the prints was entirely nature. "Beneath the Waves off Kanagawa" is painted from a low visual point so that even the backs of the waves can be seen; the striking composition is true Hokusai. The white part of the waves utilizes the natural color of the paper. "Wind in Clear Weather" depicts Mount Fuji in all its height, using simple coloration and composition incorporating the red of the mountain, the green of its base, and the white cloud-scudded sky.

# Ink Painting and Panoramic Landscapes

Broad landscapes became the important theme of artistic works from around the eleventh and twelfth centuries. It was, however, in the thirteenth century that a large number of such works began to be produced in earnest, due to the importation from China of ink painting techniques.

Ink painting (*suibokuga*) is a unique oriental form of artistic expression which utilizes black ink alone. Unlike the traditional style of Japanese painting (*yamatoe*), where an outline is first made with black ink and then the painting colored, ink painting employs the tones of the ink alone to express quality and mass in nature.

In both China and Japan, there had been a tradition of calligraphy utilizing brushes made from animal hair and black ink, and it was well understood that the flexibility of the brush's movement would be lost if too much ink was applied. The hair brush expresses, directly in the sensitivity of the lines drawn, the mental state of the artist, and it may be said that it in fact cannot be used to its full extent unless the artist is working at a peak of mental concentration.

Compared with works done on a basis of color, ink paintings prefer to attempt to express what lies behind the surface reality, moving toward that which is spiritual, a representation of the inner nature of the mind. In this, ink painting shares common features with those manifestations of the Zen spirit such as the stone gardens popular at the time, for they also attempted to take hold of the essence that underlies the various natural phenomena that the eye perceives.

**(Left) View of present-day Amanohashidate** Amanohashidate is famed as one of Japan's three most beautiful scenic places; what makes it so well-known is the sandbar, 3.3 kilometers long and between 40 and 110 meters wide, which extends out into the sea, having been made over thousands of years by river debris and the action of currents. We cannot in fact compare the modern view with Sesshu's painting with any success, for Sesshu was concerned with creating a work of art and so changed visual points for the sake of his creative power. Though the result was extremely realistic, Sesshu went beyond mere delineation to portray the scene with flexibility and spiritual dynamism.

**(Above)** *Amanohashidate* **Ink painting, Sesshu, early sixteenth century, Kyoto National Museum**
Sesshu (1420–1506) was the greatest of Japan's ink painters. He had been a Buddhist monk from a young age, and, showing early a great talent for drawing and painting, pursued his monkish life as an artist. In 1467 he traveled to China to study ink painting. In style, Sesshu departed from the heavily Chinese-influenced landscape paintings of his Japanese contemporaries, painting Japanese-style landscapes in an individual manner. *Amanohashidate* was based on Sesshu's own observations, and reminds us of his insatiable commitment to composition, in the sense of depth and breadth it invokes. Preferring an unfettered style, he worked to achieve a true delineation rather than try to put in too much detail. This work would appear, from its broad scale and freshness, to date from Sesshu's younger period, but in fact we know from internal evidence that it was painted sometime after the artist's eighty-second year.

# Flower and Plant Motifs in Textiles

Japan's national dress, the kimono, is distinctive for its splendor and subtlety, its fabric designs, and the high quality of its dyeing techniques. Today, though we see few innovations in a dress that has been brought to the ultimate in terms of form, fabric design and coloring, we are continually astounded by the freshness of a beauty deriving from two thousand years of tradition that nevertheless is not bound to any particular time.

Kimono fabric designs are based mainly upon natural motifs. It seems natural for the Japanese, steeped as they are in nature, and most at ease when a part of nature, to wear clothes that bear its designs. Japan as well is a country where the four seasons are very sharply delineated, and people wear, for example, kimono with designs of spring flowers in spring, and of the poetic sentiment of autumn in autumn. They intensely dislike to dress inappropriately to the motif of the season, and would never wear, for instance, a kimono bearing a design of a snow scene in summer. Fabric designs also interweave themes from traditional literature and drama into nature themes, adding layer upon layer of dimension to their beauty.

The sixteenth century saw innovative dyeing techniques added to the heightening of other skills that brought kimono to a new beauty. That period was a peak in kimono splendor. Kimono makers respecting tradition, do not lose sight of the sensibility of their own time and base their kimono designs on practical needs, yet today the kimono is essentially the same in design as it was in the sixteenth century.

(**Above**) Overgarment (*uchikake*) **with a design of Mount Mikasa and deer, Rakuto Museum, Kyoto** The *uchikake* is worn over the kimono and the *obi* (sash). It is of the same shape as the *kosode*.

(**Above**) Overgarment **with a design of water, cherry blossoms, wisteria, *yamabuki*, mandarin ducks, Rakuto Museum, Kyoto**

(**Left**) Yuzen (**hand-painted and dyed**) **kimono** (*kosode*) **with a design of running water, and wisteria on a white ground, Tokyo National Museum**

(**Bottom right**) Kimono (*kosode*) **with a cherry blossom pattern on a damask ground, Tokyo National Museum**

(Below) **Kimono (*kosode*) with a design of autumn plants on a white ground, Ogata Korin, Tokyo National Museum** Here the artist has painted a variety of autumn plants—chrysanthemums, Chinese bellflowers, pampas grass and bush clover—in black ink and light coloring on a white silk ground. The fine black lines with a hint of tension, and the chrysanthemum leaves drawn with ample black ink, portray poetically how the Japanese feel about autumn. The *kosode* (literally "short-sleeved") was worn widely in the fourteenth and fifteenth centuries, and is the ancestor of the modern kimono. Ogata Korin was born the son of a proprietor of a Kyoto textile shop, and as an artist expressed Japanese decorative art in its purest form.

# Flower and Plant Motifs in the Decorative Arts

With their sensitivity to seasonal changes and a lifestyle responsive to those changes, the Japanese applied stylized flower and plant motifs to their decorative arts, receiving from these nature-based designs a tranquility of spirit. Even arms and armor are decorated with elegant and delicate designs, though they were produced for use in war.

The decorative arts illustrated here date from the Edo period, between the seventeenth and nineteenth centuries. The flower and plant designs remind us inescapably of the continuous affection that Japanese have held for nature from ancient times to the present. Similar objects made by craftsmen today still employ virtually the same designs based on nature. The gentle and beautiful plants which decorate the works are nature itself; they manifest the special sensitivity of the Japanese which is able to find peace in natural beauty.

The brothers Ogata, Korin and Kenzan, whose works appear here, are representative artists and craftsmen of the Edo period. They carved out their own era in aesthetic history, breaking down tradition and creating original designs, by transmitting the gentleness and warmth that the Japanese feel toward nature.

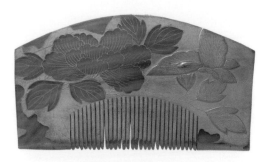

**(Above) Tortoise shell comb with gold-sprinkled lacquer (*makie*)** Ornamental combs are used by women for decorating their hair in the traditional style. Many are ornamented like this one with flowers, plants and butterflies.

**(Above) Tableware, oil paint on lacquer, plant and flower design** Oil painting on lacquer (*mitsudae*) is an oil-painting technique that was introduced early into Japan from China but hardly used after the ninth century. During the Edo period, though, it gained great popularity. The use of plant and flower designs for tableware meets with the traditional disposition of the Japanese.

**(Left) Inkstone box with *yatsuhashi* design, Ogata Korin, Tokyo National Museum** Here is another version by the same artist of the "eight bridges" design shown on p. 26. The design of the bridges and the irises matches the ground of black lacquer, to give forth a feeling of depth and elegance.

(Left) Set of five plates with designs in underglaze iron, cobalt, and overglaze gold, Ogata Kenzan, Nezu Institute of Fine Arts, Tokyo  Ogata Kenzan (1663–1743), the brother of Korin, established a kiln at Narutaki, near Kyoto, in 1689, and produced pottery into his old age. He differs from his brother in the rustic beauty of his designs.

(Left) Teabowl with a Mount Yoshino design in overglaze enamels, Nonomura Ninsei, Seikado Collection, Tokyo  Nonomura Ninsei was a ceramic artist who flourished in Kyoto in the middle of the seventeenth century. He is known for his success in devising a method for decorating his work in enamels of many colors. The decoration of a distant view of Mount Yoshino with cherry blossoms strewn about is serene and pleasant.

Round fan (*uchiwa*) with *yatsuhashi* ("eight bridges") design, Ogata Korin, Hatakeyama Museum, Tokyo  Ogata Korin (1658–1716) employed in many of his works the "eight bridges" design based on a description of a spider-web pattern of streams and the eight bridges crossing them at a place of the province of Mikawa in the ninth century "*Tales of Ise*" (*Ise Monogatari*), a collection of verse and prose by Ariwara no Narihira (825–880).  Bold and impressive is the artist's emphasis on the wooden bridges rather than the irises.

# EXPLORING JAPAN'S CULTURAL AND SCENIC TREASURES

# HOKKAIDO

Lying at the northernmost extremity of Japan, the island of Hokkaido has one distinctive feature when compared with the rest of the country. In a nation where the population is generally thickly settled, Hokkaido alone retains vast natural tracts of land. Originally the home of the Ainu, a people who are believed to share Northern Asian racial ties with the modern Japanese, Hokkaido became the focus of a full-scale development program by the Japanese government in the late nineteenth century. The retention of the region's valuable natural environment is due both to the respect that Ainu had for nature and to the comparative restraint on development imposed by Hokkaido's severe winters.

Today, Hokkaido stands as a land of hope to the average Japanese, a place to which they can escape from the narrow confines of their everyday environment and experience nature in the full. It also signifies unbounded dreams and romance, for it is a region with a rugged coastline of rocks of fantastic shapes, plains which stretch unhindered to the horizon, lakes reflecting mountains on their surfaces, a profusion of wildflowers in summer, and a promise of encounters with wild animals. It is undeniably a land filled with the delights of nature. Though there are places throughout the world where nature appears on a far greater scale, the Hokkaido scene communicates a tranquility typical of the Japanese landscape.

## The Crane

**Cranes in the Kushiro marshlands** The Kushiro marshlands of eastern Hokkaido play host between autumn and winter to a number of wintering cranes from the far north.

Broadly speaking, three species of migrating crane have been observed in Japan; those of Kushiro are known as *tancho* (Japanese crane, *Gruidae japonensis*), for their red crest.

Cranes have long been highly regarded in Japan for their delicate beauty, and at times have been thought of as messengers of the gods. As the old saying that a crane lives for a thousand years attests, the bird is honored as a symbol of longevity. The Japanese, seeing the crane soaring through the vast reaches of the sky, have imagined a celestial nymph dancing in the heavens.

## Storied Crags

**Kamui iwa (Rock of the God) at sunset.**
Along western Hokkaido stretches what has
been called the most dangerous coastline
in Japan, Cape Kamui (Kamuimisaki). Here
eroded cliffs rise more than eighty meters, and
at the shoreline are a series of rocks of fantastic
shape, of such variety that people cannot
weary of looking at them. One of these is
*kamui iwa*, a slim rock forty-one meters in
height.

There is a legend attached to this rock.
There lived in the twelfth century an ill-
starred warrior famous for his bravery, Minamoto no Yoshitsune (1159–1189), a name
familiar to all Japanese. His military skill
aroused the jealousy of his brother, the shogun
Minamoto no Yoritomo (1147–1199), and he

was forced to flee to Hokkaido. A woman
who had fallen in love with him during the
course of his journey followed him, until she
came to Cape Kamui. By the time she
arrived, though, Yoshitsune and his band had
already taken to boats and were moving out to
sea. In her grief, the woman called a curse
upon the place: "Any boat passing here carrying a woman, capsize." She then threw herself
into the sea, and became a rock, the *kamui iwa*.

History tells us that Yoshitsune was in fact
attacked and killed by his brother, and never
came to Hokkaido, so the tale must remain in
the realms of legend. Still, here where the
beauty of the sunset is exceptional, the flaming
red sky makes us think of the blaze of grief that
the woman of legend felt.

# TOHOKU

Tohoku, literally "northeast," is the northernmost region of Honshu. Lying adjacent to Hokkaido, it experiences relatively cold winters, and, because until recently it was comparatively isolated, it offers a wealth of natural beauty still untouched by urbanization.

Tohoku is also known as Michinoku, the "back roads." As far as the inhabitants of Kyoto, the seat of the central government, were concerned, it was a frontier region, beyond the regular routes. The ancient inhabitants of the area were called Emishi or Ezo. They long resisted submitting to the central authority and it was not until the twelfth century that they were brought finally under its control. This unyielding spirit long remained a local predisposition.

With such a history, Tohoku was shadowed by a harsh image. The natural environment seemed equally wild to the urban observer. That in itself, though, drew poets attracted to a type of natural beauty not to be found in the region of the capital. Matsuo Basho (1644–1694), one of Japan's most famous haiku poets, traveled in the region for five months in 1689, and has left us with a record of his journey in prose and haiku called *Oku no hosomichi* (Narrow Road to the Deep North). Even today, Tohoku retains the fascination of the "back roads."

## The Temples of Michinoku

**The five-storied pagoda at Mount Haguro**
Part of Japan's Buddhist tradition is an ascetic sect called Shugendo, whose practitioners, known as *yamabushi*, undergo their religious training in the vastnesses of mountains. In Yamagata Prefecture, in the southwestern part of Tohoku, there is a Shugendo complex consisting of three temples on three neighboring peaks, known collectively as Dewa Sanzan. Today, the principal complex is on Mount Haguro. In fact the mountain in its entirety is temple precincts, and near the path that winds up to the summit, standing amid rows of cryptomerias, is a six-hundred-year-old pagoda, a National Treasure.

The pagoda, at the base of whose central pillar are buried relics of the Buddha, has become a symbol of the temple as a whole. The five layers of roofs, tapering inward as they go up, have a serene and dignified effect. Pagodas housing the Buddha's relics are also to be found in India and China, but nowhere else outside Japan is to be found this type of five-storied pagoda. Nestled among the green leaves, the pagoda fills visitors with a bracing religious sentiment.

**The Golden Hall of Chusonji (interior)**
Eight hundred years ago in the town of Hiraizumi in Iwate Prefecture, in the eastern part of Tohoku, there flourished a magnificent culture. At that time the region was a noted producer of gold, as well as a supplier of the horses needed for battle, and Hiraizumi was at its center. There are even some historians who refer to Hiraizumi as a kingdom.

The rulers of this kingdom were a family of landed magnates called the Fujiwara, descendants of an offshoot of the powerful Kyoto family, which had left the capital to seek its fortune in the provinces. Fujiwara prosperity was brought to an end in the last years of the

twelfth century by the forces of the new shogun at Kamakura, Minamoto no Yoritomo. The great vitality of the semi-independent region disappeared overnight like a phantom.

Today the Golden Hall of Chusonji (temple) remains as a reminder of the prosperity and splendor of those few generations of glory. A National Treasure, the hall is covered by a protective building made of concrete. The interior glitters with the gold of Buddhist statues and accouterments. We are liable to think of a frontier culture based on gold as barbaric, but at Hiraizumi we see a high culture based on the aristocratic traditions of Kyoto.

## Delighting in the Beauty of Snow

**(Left) Snowscape on the Mogami river**
The Mogami is a long river which empties into the Japan Sea at Sakata in Yamagata Prefecture. Before railways were extended to this area, it was a major means of transporting rice and other goods, and during the time of its greatest prosperity, more than three hundred boats were said to be plying its waters.

Matsuo Basho took a boat down the river in 1689, commented that "there were many dangerous places" along it, and commemorated the event with a famous haiku.

> Gathering together the summer rains,
> How swift it is.
> The Mogami river.

Its role as an artery of communication now superseded, the river seen here clothed in snow, seems desolate, but that is in itself part of the fascination of Tohoku. In recent years, roofed boats have pulled out into the river on snowy days, and the passengers drink and enjoy the snowy scenery. The thick-falling snow is for the Japanese, like the cherry blossoms of spring and the russet leaves of autumn, an aspect of the beauty of nature that should be experienced.

**(Above) The Hot Spring at Ginzan** Ginzan is a small hot spring located in the mountains near Obanazawa in Yamagata Prefecture. The spring, gushing out of a river, was discovered early in the sixteenth century by miners working at the nearby silver mines. They made a simple tub and came there to bathe.

The remains of the silver mines can still be seen, and there are waterfalls and gorges nearby. Visitors enjoy eating wild vegetables and mushrooms and entering into the rustic atmosphere, with the result that the settlement is busy the year around. The area is well-known for its heavy falls of snow in winter. It is a form of spritual cleansing to warm oneself in the hot spring on a cold day, watching the surroundings turn white as the quietly falling snow conceals the dirt and grime around one.

## Local Festivals

(**Above**) **Namahage:** In Akita Prefecture, groups of two or three men wearing demon masks visit houses on the evening of December 31. They call out to the children, "Is there anyone here who cries? Anyone who doesn't do what their parents tell them? If there is, we're going to take them away with us!" and prance around fiercely. Nowadays, "namahage" has come to mean demons who go around punishing the lazy (*namakemono*), but originally it referred to the god who comes to announce the approaching New Year.

(**Right**) **Kamakura:** In February in Yokote, Akita Prefecture, holes are gouged out of piles of hardened snow to make rooms (*kamakura*), and straw mats and blankets laid down inside. Children then go in, roast *mochi* (rice cakes) to eat, and drink warmed sweet *sake*. In this area, water becomes scarce when snow falls, so that inside the snow hut there is always an altar with offerings to the water god.

36

(**Above**) **Chaguchagu umako:** In June, farmers of Iwate Prefecture decorate their horses and take them in a slow procession which lasts around four hours along a route of fifteen kilometers. Before the mechanization of agriculture, the horse was a vital force in farming. The festival was instituted out of the love farmers had for their horses, to give the hard-working horses one day's well-earned rest, and to make a pilgrimage to the shrine of the horse god.

(**Above**) **Kanto:** The Kanto (Lantern) Festival is held in Akita City in August. Men balance thick bamboo poles strung with tens of lighted lanterns on cross-poles on their shoulders and even on their jaws without using their hands, to the accompaniment of shouts of encouragement. Like the Nebuta, the Kanto Festival originated in an exorcism of evil spirits and prayers for continuing good health.

**Nebuta:** The Nebuta Festival, held in Aomori City in August, is famous for enormous paper floats featuring representations of warrior faces. The floats are constructed of paper pasted over a framework of bamboo, wood, and wire. At night, lanterns are lit from inside, and the huge, shining, warrior faces are led in procession through warm summer streets, accompanied by large numbers of revelers dancing in rhythm, creating an overwhelming impression. The festival was originally held to exorcise evil, disease-bringing spirits, and to pray for continuing good health.

# KANTO

The Kanto region, containing the nation's capital, Tokyo, occupies a corner of the southeastern part of Central Honshu. Though it comprises a little under 10% of Japan's total area, it is home to 30% of its population, the political, economic, and cultural hub of the nation.

Climatically, Kanto is more moderate than Hokkaido or Tohoku, but even so there is considerable variety from area to area. The coastal regions are warm, while the mountainous areas are comparatively colder. In between mountains and sea stretches the Kanto Plain, the most extensive in Japan.

In the mountains, Nikko and Ozegahara are well-known tourist attractions, while the Suigo area, on the plain near the sea, draws many visitors. Tokyo and Kamakura are famous for their historical connections.

The Kanto has traditionally been thought of as a region of warrior power. When at the end of the twelfth century Minamoto no Yoritomo established his shogunate, the first example of independent warrior administration in Japan's history, it was at Kamakura. Then in the seventeenth century, when Tokugawa Ieyasu (1542–1616) became shogun, setting up the third instance of warrior administration, he based himself in Edo, the modern Tokyo. Only the second shogunate, that brought into being by Ashikaga Takauji (1305–1358) in the fourteenth century, was in the old capital, Kyoto, but even so, Takauji himself hailed from the present Tochigi Prefecture in northern Kanto.

The inhabitants of Kyoto would have looked upon the Kanto warriors as wild and uncouth though militarily strong. The natural surroundings of the region are likewise not as gentle as those of Kyoto and invoke feelings of a certain simple affection.

# NIKKO

Nikko is in the northern part of the Kanto region, a cultural center well-known to visitors from all over the world. Twelve hundred years ago it was a sacred center for the mountain cult, and today a number of temples and shrines—Rinnoji, Toshogu, Futarasan Jinja—stand nestled among tall trees. Somewhat away from the town is the ninety-four meter Kegon Falls, which with the Toshogu Shrine is a must on the tourist itinerary.

### *A Magnificence of Shrines*

**The Yomeimon (Gate of Sunlight) at Toshogu Shrine** The Toshogu Shrine was built to enshrine the spirit of the first Tokugawa shogun, Ieyasu. Its beautiful buildings, decorated with large numbers of carvings, decorative paintings, and metal fittings, were completed in 1636. The centerpiece of the complex is the famous gate, Yomeimon, with a frontage of seven meters and a height of eleven meters. There is hardly a space on the gate that is not covered with gilded or painted carvings, some four hundred in number. The Japanese call it by a nickname, Higurashi-mon (the twilight gate), implying that we could spend the whole day looking at it without tiring.

No one can help being surprised by the splendor of the gate. It was erected at enormous expense by Tokugawa Iemitsu (1604–1651), the

third shogun, out of reverence for his grandfather, Ieyasu. Traditional tenets of beauty in Japan tend toward the elegant and understated, as typified by Kyoto culture. Seen in this light, the flamboyant colors of the Yomeimon are of a different culture, that of the powerful warrior class as opposed to the aristocratic culture of Kyoto. And so, such splendid beauty has to be considered part also of Japanese aesthetics.

# TOKYO

Situated in the southern part of the Kanto region, Tokyo, with a population of more than ten million, is one of the largest cities in the world. The capital of Japan, it is also the center of its economy, culture and information network. In this dynamic city blend the cultures of East and West, and the old and the new exist side by side.

Tokyo has been Japan's center since the seventeenth century, when Tokugawa Ieyasu became shogun and established his government there. Even after the fall of the shogunate in the second half of the nineteenth century, Tokyo remained, in fact as well as in name, the nation's capital, when the emperor moved there from Kyoto.

Compared with the thousand or more years of history that is Kyoto, Tokyo is a young city. Nevertheless, you have only to move away from the government and business centers, and from districts popular with the young like Roppongi, Harajuku and Aoyama, and set your steps toward the eastern parts of the city to find a three-hundred-year-old history alive in the old, commoners' suburbs.

## *The Imperial Palace*

(**Above**) **Nijubashi** The bridge in front of the main entrance to the Imperial Palace is its symbol. The modern bridge, built in 1887, exudes a quiet solemnity. Nijubashi (Double Bridge) receives its name from its two spans, one over the deep moat at water level, and the other high above it.

(**Left**) **The Fushimi watchtower and rampart** The Imperial Palace, the residence of the emperor, is built on the site of the old Edo Castle, whose remains are still to be seen here and there. One such is the Fushimi watchtower, brought to Edo from Fushimi, near Kyoto, in 1628.

(**Below**) **The flower-strewn banks of the Palace moat** Most of the Imperial Palace is surrounded by a moat, the home of white swans. On its banks, cherry trees mingle with pines and other green trees, and in spring the area is a mass of blossom, tinting the solemn walls of the Palace a vivid color.

## *The Old Areas of Tokyo*

**(Above left) The Sanja Festival of Asakusa**
Asakusa is the best known of Tokyo's old plebeian districts. At its center is the temple Sensoji, crowded with visitors the year around, whose numbers top twenty million annually. Here in May is held the Sanja Festival. "Sanja" (literally "three shrines") refers to the three men who are connected with the foundation of the temple.

During the festival, more than one hundred portable shrines (*mikoshi*) from local districts are brought out and shouldered through the streets of Asakusa to the accompaniment of shouts and chants. This animated popular festival retains the traditions of the time when Tokyo was still Edo.

**(Above right) The Kaminarimon**   Passing under this "Thunder Gate," visitors make their way to Sensoji, which looms at the end of the narrow street. On either side of the gate stand carved figures of the thunder god (from whom comes its name) and the wind god. The enormous lantern hanging down from the roof of the gate is a reminder of the past for us.

**(Right) Tori no ichi**   Tori no ichi is a festival held in November at the Otori Shrine in Asakusa. In the past, the Japanese divided the days of the month according to the twelve signs of the zodiac, which were given animal names, and one such was the Day of the Cock (*tori*). Long ago in the mythological age, a hero by the name of Yamato Takeru no Mikoto was said to have announced a victory in battle to the gods of this shrine on the Day of the Cock in November, and so the festival began. It is more likely though to have been originally an agricultural festival marking the end of the rice harvest which later became transmuted into a festival for commercial prosperity.

Visitors to the festival buy colorfully decorated rakes (*kumade*) which are considered auspicious. From the teeth of the rake hang a great many symbols of good luck and fertility. Buyers hope that they will thereby be able to "rake" in riches and good fortune.

## Theaters of the Classical Arts

The three pillars of Japanese traditional theater are Kabuki, Noh and Bunraku. Tokyo, providing for the classical arts as well as the most modern forms of culture, has venues for all three.

**(Below) A performance of the Kabuki play "Gohiiki kanjincho"** Of all the Kabuki plays, "Kanjincho" is the nearest to the Western theatrical tradition in terms of plot. The word "kabuki" originally meant "out of the ordinary," and Kabuki contains therefore many fantastic plots. Characteristic of Kabuki is the exotic red makeup symbolizing bravery (see the actor in the photo) and an overstated acting style. Since women do not appear at all, men play women's roles (these are called *oyama*). Kabuki gives its audience a sense of the extraordinary.

**(Above) The Kabukiza (exterior)** One of the sights of Tokyo, the Kabukiza, is a commercial theater which specializes in performances of Kabuki, held for most of the year. It was built in 1889 as part of the government's movement to modernize the theater, and has been burned down since three times: once through a short-circuit, and later in the Great Earthquake of 1923 and during wartime bombing. The present building dates from 1951. Externally the theater incorporates many architectural features of the late sixteenth century, but inside the facilities are completely modern.

**(Above) The Noh stage at the National Noh Theater** The National Noh Theater was opened in September 1983, the only national one in the country. It provides opportunities for people to enjoy Noh performances, and has facilities for training and research. On the backdrop of a Noh stage is a depiction of a pine tree, and this never changes, whatever the play being performed. The performers enter the stage from the left.

**(Right) A performance of the Noh play "Hagoromo"** Noh has a venerable history stretching back to the fourteenth century, thus predating both Kabuki and Bunraku (seventeenth century). Being performed by masked actors, Noh emphasizes passing beyond the everyday world into a realm of the surreal. It sheds light on those dark places deep in the human psyche and penetrates deep into the inner lives of its protagonists. In expression, it is rich in abstract symbolism, and reveals characteristics of a Japanese aesthetic consciousness rich in elegance and subtlety.

**(Right) A performance of the Bunraku play "Sonezaki shinju"** Perhaps one of the most famous plays written for the puppet theater, *Sonezaki shinju* (Love Suicide at Sonezaki) tells of two lovers, who, unable to marry in this world, resolve on suicide. Here they stand together on a bridge, on their way to their final destination in some nearby woods. Bunraku became part of the Japanese theatrical tradition in the seventeenth and eighteenth centuries, thanks largely to the genius of the playwright Chikamatsu Monzaemon (1653–1724), who depicted with great tenderness in his work the tragedy of a man and woman who tried to find a solution to their love amid the pressures and contradictions of a feudal society.

Three puppeteers manipulate the puppets—the main one called *omozukai* who controls the head and the right arm, a subordinate, the *hidaritezukai* who works the left arm, and *ashizukai* who is in charge of the legs. The puppet, normally devoid of facial expression, is somehow given life by the puppeteers, who succeed in expressing warm emotions in their puppets and in creating a beauty unobtainable in a human performance.

# KAMAKURA

With Kyoto and Nara, Kamakura is known around the world as a place of history and culture. The hitherto lonely farming and fishing village moved onto the stage of history in 1192 when the new shogun, Minamoto no Yoritomo, established his government there. Facing the sea on its south side, it nestles at the foot of hills in the other three directions, and is a rolling, verdant town. About fifty years ago, it became popular to build summer villas in the hilly parts of Kamakura, and this area has now turned into a quiet, quality residential district. With temples over seven hundred years old and many other historical sites, Kamakura is a popular one-day trip from Tokyo.

## *A Great Buddha Seated amid the Dew*

(**Above right**) **The Great Buddha of Kamakura** The Great Buddha is eleven meters tall, the second largest in Japan after the Great Buddha at Todaiji in Nara. It was originally constructed of wood, but very soon remade in bronze. We do not know exactly when it was built, but scholars think it was sometime in the latter half of the thirteenth century. It was originally housed in a special hall, but this was destroyed by storms twice during the fourteenth century and demolished by a tidal wave in 1495. Thus the Great Buddha has remained out in the open for the past five hundred years.

The statue is hollow inside, and visitors can enter through a small door in the side, climb a staircase, and peep out of the two windows at the back. We feel awe when we look at Buddhist statues inside a dim temple, but seeing the Great Buddha seated beneath the vault of the sky we find it easy to feel the statue as a friendly presence. That is perhaps why the Great Buddha is so popular. Throughout the year it is visited by a never-ending stream of students on schooltrips and by tourists, and is the virtual symbol of Kamakura.

(**Right**) **Yabusame at Hachiman Shrine**
*Yabusame* is an archery contest conducted on horseback, and was a popular pastime among Kamakura warriors between the twelfth and fourteenth centuries. It is now held every September at the Hachiman Shrine, enabling us to recall the splendors of Kamakura during the age of the warriors.

(**Right**) **Hydrangeas at Meigetsuin**    In the thirteenth century, Meigetsuin was a large temple, but now it has shrunk considerably in size.   Bordering the path leading to the main temple building are thousands of hydrangea bushes, which have given Meigetsuin its nickname of "Hydrangea Temple."   When the flowers bloom, from the beginning to the middle of June, long streams of people emerge from the station at North Kamakura to see the glorious display.

47

# CHUBU

The Chubu region of Central Honshu can be divided geographically and climatically into three sub-regions. The area to the north overlooking the Sea of Japan is called Hokuriku; at its center is the famous castle town of Kanazawa, a cultural hub. Historically the ties between Kanazawa and Kyoto have been strong, with the result that a cultural elegance is characteristic of Kanazawa. The surrounding region has one of the heaviest snowfalls in Japan; irrigated by the waters of the melting snow, the land is the premier rice-producing area of Japan.

Further south on the Pacific side, the climate is mild, suiting agriculture. Its principal city, Nagoya, with a population of over two million, is Japan's fourth largest, and is developing as an industrial center.

Between these two sub-regions there are the central highlands, where tall mountains in the three thousand meter range soar. From their similarity in shape to the European Alps, they have come to be called the Japan Alps, the "roof of Japan." Unspoiled by urbanization, this area retains its natural beauty and the traditions of the old mountain communities.

Snow and mountains ensure that Chubu is chock-full of scenic attractions. Wherever you go, there are the delights of nature and history, and it is not surprising that tourists, hikers and mountain climbers flock here the year around.

## Eiheiji and Kenrokuen

**(Left) The Chokushimon (Imperial Messenger's Gate) of Eiheiji** Eiheiji is one of the most important Zen training temples in Japan, maintaining the traditions of the teachings of the Soto school of Zen that Dogen (1200–1253) brought back from China some seven hundred years ago. The impressive, hushed precincts of more than 330,000 sq. m. are covered by tall stands of cryptomerias, some more than six hundred years old.

The temple does not encourage sightseeing for its own sake, but urges overnight visitors to look on their stay as a form of religious training. They are awakened at five a.m. in winter, and four a.m. in summer to attend the early morning meditation session. Conversation is forbidden during mealtimes and in the bath, and visitors are expected to observe the Buddhist precepts.

The Chokushimon is the gate used only when the temple is visited by an imperial messenger. On the great doors is placed the imperial crest, the chrysanthemum.

**Kenrokuen in autumn and winter** Kenrokuen, a landscape garden constructed in the *kaiyu* (strolling garden) style by the feudal lord of Kanazawa in the latter part of the seventeenth century, is located in the center of the city. It recreates natural scenery through the use of such devices as ponds, pine trees, and cherry trees. One of the most noted gardens in the country, it is perhaps the best of the daimyo (feudal lord) gardens in terms of its quintessential Japanese elegance and beauty. The stone lanterns placed in the middle of the pond are impressive, and are a favorite background for the photographs taken by visitors. Spring is characterized by cherry blossoms, azaleas, and irises, autumn by bush clover and russet leaves, and winter by a snow-covered landscape of trees and lanterns.

Opposite the garden is the site of the old Kanazawa Castle. It is a neighborhood redolent of an atmosphere of the past.

## Surviving Traditions of the Mountain Country

**(Below) The daimyo's inn at Tsumago**
During the Tokugawa period, Tsumago was a post station along the Nakasendo, the old inland route linking Edo and Kyoto. Here the pre-nineteenth century townscape has been restored on a large scale, so that visitors walking the streets have the illusion of having slipped through a time tunnel to the world of two hundred years ago. Restoration has not meant the aridity of a film set; rather, as in Takayama, the town is a living setting for the everyday lives of its inhabitants.

Post stations contained inns for ordinary travelers, as well as special accommodation, called *honjin* or *wakihonjin*, for the daimyo (feudal lords) journeying to and from the capital. The photograph shows the interior of the *honjin* at Tsumago. The floors are covered with straw matting (*tatami*), and in a hearth in the center of the room a fire gives out warmth. The heavy beams of the ceiling allow us to understand how solidly Japanese houses were constructed.

Today, the building is a local history museum, and anyone can enter and rest inside.

**(Above) Roadside *dosojin* (stone statues of gods)** A common site on the roadsides of the Azumino district in the Northern Alps (Hida Range) of Nagano Prefecture are small stone statues of a pair of figures, male and female. These are called *dosojin*.

The *dosojin* were originally placed on the borders of villages as deities to keep out the evil spirits that brought disease and calamity. Held in affection by the villagers, they came to be associated with marriage, and so were often depicted as a loving couple. Recipients of the simple prayers of common people, they bring peace of mind to the passer-by.

**Houses at Shirakawago** Two villages in the northwest of Gifu Prefecture, Shirakawa and Shokawa (previously Shirakawago), are at the center of an area famous for the steep-roofed farmhouses seen in the photograph. The roofs were pitched at an angle of sixty degrees to cope with heavy winter snows. They are unusual in Japanese wooden architecture in that they are built on a large scale with three or four stories. The severe climate of the region forced people to work indoors, so ample working and sleeping areas for an extended family had to be provided.

# KINKI

Today the political and cultural center of Japan is Tokyo, the hub of the Kanto region. For more than a thousand years, though, this position was occupied by the Kinki region, centering on Nara and Kyoto. In the course of its long history it was many times the portal for entry of advanced cultures from the Asian mainland. There is no region in Japan more deeply imbued with historical tradition, and we must consider it the heart of Japanese culture and aesthetics.

The ancient cities of Nara and Kyoto, whose histories date back to the seventh and eighth centuries, Ise, the shrine of the imperial ancestral deities, and Osaka, Japan's third largest city established more than four hundred years ago, all belong to the Kinki region. The Yamato area, of which Nara is the center, is a cradle of the two-thousand-year-old Japanese culture. A poem in the ancient historical chronicle called the *Kojiki* (Record of Ancient Matters) reads:

> "Yamato is a fine land;
> Nestling among mountains,
> Folded layer upon layer,
> A green wall.
> How beautiful is Yamato!"

The gentle environment supported the first flourishing of ancient culture and today still contains a large number of temples and shrines. Yamato is the heartland of Japanese beauty and sentiment.

## Abodes of the Gods

**(Left) The Wedded Rocks of Futamigaura** The area where the Isuzu river, which flows through the Inner Shrine of Ise, empties into the Bay of Ise is called Futamigaura. In the old days sea salt was produced here for the Ise Shrine and it was a domain of that shrine. Further, it was a custom for pilgrims to the shrine to purify themselves by bathing in the sea here and the district flourished as a result. In the sea at Futamigaura there are

two rocks joined by a sacred straw rope called *shimenawa*, the so-called "wedded rocks." The straw rope is used in Shinto to set apart that which is considered sacred. It is an emotional experience to witness the morning sun rising over the wedded rocks, for it is easy to imagine that it is the Sun God making a brilliant appearance in the world. People pack the area on New Year's Day to see the first sunrise of the year behind the rocks.

## The Inner Shrine of Ise, main building

The Ise Shrine venerates the deities considered the imperial ancestors and, with Izumo Grand Shrine, is Japan's oldest and most highly regarded shrine. Worshipped at the Inner Shrine is Amaterasu Omikami, the mythical ancestral deity of the imperial family, and at the Outer Shrine Toyouke Okami, the god of food, clothing and housing. The two shrines are some five kilometers apart, but both are surrounded by thick forest, and the skillful blending of stone and wood leaves a lasting impression on the minds of visitors, drawing them into the realm of the mystical.

The main building of the Inner Shrine is ancient architecture in its pristine form, and makes the most of natural building materials. Its simple lineal beauty reminds us strongly of its age and sanctity. Such simplicity is the wellspring of Japanese beauty. This building has been reconstructed every twenty years since ancient times. Its next reconstruction will be in 1993.

## Mountain Temples

**(Left) The Nachi Waterfall and the three-storied pagoda of Mount Nachi** The whole of the southern part of the Kii Ranges in Southern Kinki is known as Kumano. Though the mountains there are not particularly high, the far peaks were in the past rarely visited by urban dwellers, and became associated with Shugendo and its mountain practitioners. Therefore, Kumano has been a religious site from ancient times and is known today for three large and important shrines, collectively called "Kumano Sanzan." One of them, Kumano Nachi Taisha, originally had no main sanctuary, for the Nachi waterfall itself, in a primeval forest of cryptomeria and cypress, was the god venerated. The waterfall is 133 meters in height, the largest in Japan. Pilgrims forget the cares of the world as they look at and listen to the waterfall.

**(Above) The Inner Sanctuary of Koyasan** Koyasan is the temple founded by the great religious figure Kobo Daishi (Kukai, 774–835) after his return from study in China early in the ninth century. He deliberately built his temple deep in the mountains far away from urban settlement, for he deplored the strong ties that bound Buddhism and the aristocratic governing class. The Inner Sanctuary is in the most remote part of the temple precincts. There is a long avenue extending for some two kilometers which leads up to Kukai's tomb. On either side of the avenue are the graves of more than 200,000 people, nameless as well as famous. Even at midday the surroundings are dark, because of the shade of the many ancient cryptomerias. Even those who have no understanding of Buddhism at all cannot help but feel something profound and mysterious here. Koyasan reveals to us another aspect of classical Japanese beauty.

# KYOTO

Kyoto has flourished as Japan's heart for more than a thousand years since its foundation in 794. Its rich store of history and tradition is matched by its enviable cultural elegance. Most of what we know today as Japanese aesthetics originated in Kyoto. Kyoto's historical and cultural heritage belongs not only to Japan but to all humanity. For this reason perhaps, Kyoto was not bombed during the Second World War, by the deliberate policy of the American military authorities.

Kyoto suffers severe winters and humid summers. By contrast, spring and autumn are moderate and pleasant. Perhaps such a contrast of seasons gave rise to a love of nature and the need to search for beauty within nature. Large numbers of temples, gardens and old dwellings remain in Kyoto. Traditional crafts such as weaving and ceramics are popular, and special festivals and events dot the calendar.

Kyoto's fame draws visitors from around the world, but for the Japanese, the city is like their heart's home. Often they can be heard to say amid the grind of everyday life how they would like to be spending a leisurely time in Kyoto, taking in the sights.

## Gold, Silver and Stone

(**Above**) **The stone garden of Ryoanji**  The stone garden of Ryoanji is one of Japan's most famous gardens. An earthen wall borders the rectangular garden to the east, south and west. The surface of the garden is completely covered with white sand, on which are placed fifteen stones in groups of seven, five and three from east to west. The fifteen cannot all be seen at one time, for they have been so designed that at least one is hidden, from whichever angle the visitor looks. It is said that the sand represents the sea, and the rocks islands floating on its waves. Such awareness that the whole world may be found in a small space, that the action of the universe is apparent in a small event, is the fundamental spirit of Zen. What has become the basis of Japanese aesthetic consciousness, to bring about a feeling of quietness and tranquility, made its appearance around the fourteenth century.

**(Left) The Golden Pavilion** The third Muromachi shogun, Ashikaga Yoshimitsu (1358–1408), retired to his mountain villa in the Kitayama district of Kyoto after handing over his titles to his son in 1397. This villa was what became the Golden Pavilion; as its name sugests, its walls were covered in gold leaf. It is three-storied, each floor of a different architectural style. The first has elements of an aristocratic residence (*shinden* style), the second a warrior's residence (*buke* style) and the third a Zen temple. This very much reflects the eclecticism of the period, when the three cultures of aristocrat, warrior and Zen were intertwined. Here is splendor amid dignity. Carefully preserved over the centuries, the Golden Pavilion sadly was burned down in 1950 by a young priest jealous of the building's beauty. It was restored and rebuilt five years later. Yukio Mishima's novel, *The Golden Pavilion*, was based upon this episode. The gold leaf was replaced in 1987, bringing back the pavilion's original beauty.

**(Left) The Silver Pavilion** The eighth Muromachi shogun, Ashikaga Yoshimasa (1436–1490), built the Silver Pavilion in 1489 in the Higashiyama district of Kyoto after he yielded his rule to his son. In an attempt to imitate the Golden Pavilion, he is reputed to have intended to have the building covered in silver leaf, but what exactly happened remains unclear. The pavilion has two stories, the lower the earliest example of the newly evolving Japanese domestic architectural style (*shoin*), and the upper in the Zen style. The Golden Pavilion had been built at the zenith of the Ashikaga shogunate, while the Silver Pavilion was erected at a time of its decline, when Japan had begun to fall into unrest and civil war. Yoshimasa, deliberately trying to take refuge from the hostilities of his time, sought at the Silver Pavilion to immerse himself in beauty and the arts. To this extent, the pavilion was an expression of a purified Japanese aesthetic. Spurning surface show, Yoshimasa sought beauty in the ultimate refinement of simplicity. This ideal penetrated people's aesthetic consciousness on a wide scale in a variety of aspects, and so had a great influence on Japanese tradition.

## Katsura Rikyu

(Above) **View from the Gepparo** The Katsura Detached Palace was built for Prince Toshihito (1579–1629), the younger brother of Emperor Goyozei, between the years 1620 and 1629. Its seven main structures are placed around a pond made of water drawn from the nearby Katsura river, a pond which is located virtually in the center of a 10,000 square meter site surrounded by bamboo groves. In the past, guests surveyed the buildings from boats floating on the pond, but now visitors rather walk quietly around the garden. Each ornamental stone is carefully positioned to achieve a subtle aesthetic sense. The superb harmony between the beauty of architecture and garden cannot be surpassed.

It was Bruno Taut (1880–1938), a German architect who came to Japan in 1933, who extolled the "eternal" beauty of the Katsura Detached Palace. Moved himself by the mixture of functionalism and aestheticism in Japanese architecture, he made its beauty known to the world.

**The principal structure** The central building of the Palace, on the west side of the pond, consists of three sections in the *shoin* (residential) style, the Old Shoin, the Middle Shoin and the New Shoin. Each wing is built at a slightly different angle to make the most of the sunlight. Balance between high and low, small and large, is carefully attained, and the whole resembles a single structure. Floors are raised to keep the building free from moisture,

those of each wing being a step higher than the others. The small differences can be discerned in the external view. The contrasting black and white tones of the walls achieve a simple beauty without the need for decoration. The Palace is regarded as the best example of Japanese traditional architecture, in terms of the fusing of practical craftsmanship and a delicate sense of beauty.

## Palace and Castle

**Kyoto Imperial Palace    The Shishinden (above) and the Kurodo no ma of the Seiryoden (below)**    During the period that Kyoto was Japan's capital (794–1868), the Imperial Palace was the residence of the Emperor and the center of affairs of state. The palace has been burned down and reconstructed many times; the present buildings date from the reconstruction of 1856 which attempted to imitate as closely as possible the Heian style of palace architecture. The Shishinden (Pure Dragon Hall) was the main hall used for important ceremonies, and the Seiryoden (Pure Cool Hall) was where the Emperor lived.

The Imperial Palace is wooden, and of the utmost simplicity. Historically, the Japanese emperors have been religious leaders, praying to heaven for the peace of the nation, rather than warriors who have dominated the people through force. They tended to dislike the flamboyant, that redolent of the power of riches, and preserved a quiet and simple aesthetic consciousness evocative of spiritual depth.

**The Ohiroma (Grand Chamber) of Nijo Castle, Kyoto**    Tokugawa Ieyasu began building Nijo Castle as his Kyoto residence in 1602, a short time before he became shogun. The Ohiroma was where the shogun would receive the greatest of the feudal lords in audience, sitting on the slightly raised platform at the back of the room, called the *jodan no ma*, the upper portion.

The ceiling is richly decorated in its entirety, and surrounded by large paintings of pine

trees on a gilt background. For a military leader who had brought peace to the warring country through force, a room had to portray his might and authority, and so needed to be splendidly decorated. This attitude contrasts with the aesthetic consciousness found portrayed in the Kyoto Imperial Palace.

Though the pine trees in the paintings are enormous, they are of simple composition, characteristic of the traditional Japanese aesthetic.

## Festivals and Observances

(**Left**) **Kotohajime** Kotohajime ("the initial ritual") on December 13 marks the beginning of preparations for the New Year. Today it takes the form solely of a ritual greeting by Gion *maiko* (entertainers) to their dancing teachers to express their thanks for the guidance they have received over the past year. *Maiko* are young girls who perform traditional dances at places of entertainment, the oldest and most high class of these being in Kyoto's Gion quarter. Their costume, seen in the photograph, reflects the style worn by the daughters of rich merchant families in the past.

(**Below left**) **Mifune Festival** The Mifune ("three boats") festival is held on the Oi river at Arashiyama on the third Sunday of May. At this time, boats resembling the pleasure craft used by the nobility a thousand years ago are launched, carrying dancers and musicians playing traditional instruments. The "three boats" refer to those carrying the best poet in the ancient Chinese style, the best poet in the Japanese (*waka*) style, and the best musician. In the past the emperor would designate certain boats for his own pleasure. Today, the festival features a variety of boats with different performers.

(**Above**) **Kemari hajime** "Kemari" is a traditional game somewhat resembling football in which a ball has to be kicked from participant to participant without touching the ground. It was brought to Japan from China in the eighth century and became popular among the aristocracy. It is a spectacle rather than a sport and the players wear elegant robes and leather boots to kick the leather ball (see photograph). The tradition has been preserved in a ritual at the Shimogamo Shrine in Kyoto, called "Kemari hajime" ("the first kemari"), which takes place on January 4.

**(Above) Aoi Festival**   The Aoi (Hollyhock) Festival is held at the Kamo Shrine (Kamigamo and Shimogamo Shrines) each year on May 15. People in the costumes of the aristocracy of a thousand years ago pull *gissha* (ox-carts), in which the ancient nobility used to ride, through the streets of Kyoto to the shrine. The festival's origins go back more than fourteen hundred years to a time when the harvest was ruined by continual wind and rain.   The emperor therefore sent a messenger to the Kamo Shrine to perform rites for a return to normal seasons.   Since then it became the custom for the emperor to send a messenger with a retinue to the shrine every year, an event now known as the Kamo Festival.   It is popularly called the Hollyhock Festival because hollyhock leaves, believed to be efficacious in averting lightning and earthquakes, are used for decoration.

**(Right) Gion Festival**   The Gion Festival of the Yasaka Shrine in Gion lasts for much of the month of July, but its highlight is on July 17, when a parade of gorgeously decorated floats (*yamaboko*) winds slowly through the city streets.   The festival originated in the ninth century during a severe epidemic to pacify the spirits thought causing the disease.   The Gion Festival has now come to be thought of as the epitome of Kyoto's festivals, and of Japan's, and it attracts more than a million spectators each year. Supported in the past by the townspeople, and still sustained by the enthusiasm of the citizens of Kyoto with pride in Japan's traditions, the Gion Festival enchants people from all over the world.

### The Paradise of Uji

**The Phoenix Hall of Byodoin**　Byodoin, once the villa of the great eleventh century statesman Fujiwara no Michinaga (966–1027), was made a temple in 1053 by Michinaga's son, Yorimichi (992–1074).　The main structure is the Phoenix Hall, a National Treasure, designed to resemble a phoenix with outstretched

wings. By the time Yorimichi succeeded his father, the golden age of aristocratic government had begun to decline and shadows were falling across society. Perhaps for this reason, Yorimichi was seized by anxiety and, predicting the ruin of society as he had known it, determined to construct an earthly paradise as an escape. This was the Phoenix Hall. Seated in the front part of the Hall is a statue of Amida (Amitabha), the Buddha who has vowed to lead all to his Western Paradise of the Pure Land. On the ceiling and the upper walls are painted a number of small Buddhas riding on clouds. The doors and walls are brightly painted with scenes of Amida descending to welcome the dead to his paradise. Both the building and its surrounding garden express the theme of an earthly paradise.

# NARA

Nara is, with Kyoto and Kamakura, one of Japan's best known historical cities. From 710 to 784 it was the capital of Japan. A poem in the Manyoshu, the oldest Japanese anthology of poetry, extols the city, saying,

> "The Imperial City, Nara the green,
> Blooms now like flowers
> At the height of their beauty."

For a few short decades, Buddhist culture became dominant, so that today Nara has been left with a rich heritage of temples and statues. Unlike Kyoto, which remained the capital for a thousand years, and which saw a gradual growth of an elegant townscape over its entire area, Nara is today situated in verdant natural surroundings, full of unexpected discoveries of a subtle beauty in places that remain undescribed in tourist guides.

## Buddha and Pagoda

(**Above left**) **Todaiji and the Great Buddha**
Todaiji has the largest Buddha in Japan, fifteen meters in height. In 743, the Emperor Shomu ordered its construction, and after some difficulties, the statue was completed and dedicated in 752. More than ten thousand monks, including an Indian monk, and nobles attended the ceremony. This was a time of serious conflict between the various noble families, when a national system of land distribution was being brought into being. Himself uneasy, the emperor planned to use Buddhism to bring stability to the country, and therefore embarked on the vast task of accumulating the funds to construct the Great Buddha.

Despite the emperor's hopes, the Great Buddha was later burned down twice during civil wars, and the present statue is a restoration dating from the beginning of the eighteenth century. Though it is a meter shorter than the original, it is of the same form.

**Yakushiji**  The temple Yakushiji was founded in 680 in the former capital of Fujiwara (Nara Prefecture), which preceded Nara. After the capital was shifted in 710, the temple was rebuilt in the new capital, though it is not known whether the buildings and the statues in the present structure resemble the original or not.  The buildings in the photograph are, from the left, the Kondo (Golden Hall), the Western Pagoda and the Eastern Pagoda.  The two pagodas are placed opposite each other on an east-west line, with the Kondo in between. The Eastern Pagoda dates from the eighth century, and shows an elegance derived from twelve hundred years of exposure to the elements.  Ernest Fenollosa (1853–1908), the American student of fine arts who came to Japan in the late nineteenth century, described the flow of the roofs of the pagoda as "frozen music."

The brightly painted Western Pagoda was reconstructed in 1981 after 450 years.  All Buddhist temples of the time were as brightly painted when they were new; over the centuries, though, their colors have faded to the muted tones now seen in the Eastern Pagoda. Temples in China and Korea are kept painted, whereas the Japanese, preferring a natural faded appearance, rarely repaint them.  Here also is apparent the Japanese aesthetic taste for the understated.

## Horyuji, the Oldest Wooden Building in the World

**Horyuji (above, overall view, left, aerial view)** Horyuji was built here at Ikaruga by order of Prince Shotoku (574–622) thirteen hundred years ago. Originally constructed in 607, it was destroyed by lightning in 670 and later rebuilt. Even so, it is now the oldest wooden building in the world.

More than fifty halls stretch over the 130,000 square meter grounds. Of those, nineteen, including the five-storied pagoda and the Kondo (Golden Hall), are National Treasures. The temple also has numerous Buddhist statues and other works of art, 135 of which are National Treasures and 1,870 Important Cultural Properties. Horyuji is

indeed a treasure house of Japanese Buddhist art. The pagoda with its dynamic beauty is the most magical of all the buildings. It seems to move and dance depending on the angle and place it is viewed from, without losing the slightest sense of stability. Here we can see that the ancient Japanese were not bound by formality or convention, but attempted a free form.

(**Above**) **Guze Kannon**  The Guze Kannon is the principal image of the Yumedono (Hall of Dreams) in the eastern part of the precinct. It is said to be modeled after Prince Shotoku himself. It was kept hidden away for many centuries, revealed only to the monks of the temple. In 1884, Ernest Fenollosa visited Horyuji at the behest of the Ministry of Education, at which time the statue was shown to him. It is said that the temple monks fled in fear that a curse would fall upon them. Wrapped in more than ninety meters of cloth, the statue had been preserved in remarkably fine condition for thirteen hundred years. It appears at first glance to be of gilt bronze, but on closer inspection it is seen to be made of a single piece of wood, covered with gold leaf. At present, it is exhibited only at certain times in spring and autumn.

# OSAKA

For many years, just as Edo (Tokyo) was known as a city of the military class, and Kyoto as one of the aristocracy, Osaka was considered a city of merchants. This tradition remains strong; there substance is valued above form, and a spirit of rationalism and realism is strongly rooted. Osaka's rise to prosperity dates back over four hundred years, to the time when Toyotomi Hideyoshi (1536–1598), victor in the civil wars that had divided Japan for more than a century, decided to make it his chief stronghold and build up the area as a center of commerce by attracting merchants to come and dwell there. Though a military general, Hideyoshi's antecedents were among the village headman and farmer class, and therefore he was extremely popular among the common people. In that he encouraged economic development in a planned and positive way, he is a true symbol of an Osaka man.

Today, Osaka, with a population of 2.6 million, is Japan's third largest city, and the biggest center of western Japan. Furthermore, it comprises the country's second most important industrial area. Nevertheless, despite the superficial covering of a mass of modern buildings, it still throbs with the old spirit of merchants and commoners.

## *The Commoners' Castle Town*

(**Above**) **Toka Ebisu, Imamiya Ebisu Shrine**   There are many shrines in the Kinki district to Ebisu, god of business, whose festival is held on January 10, and who is therefore known as Toka (the tenth) Ebisu. Though the main festival rituals are held on the tenth, events also spill over to the ninth and the eleventh. At the Imamiya Ebisu Shrine in Osaka's Nambu district, more than a million people attend the festival over these three days. Vendors cry out greetings for business prosperity as they vie to sell *fukuzasa*, branches of bamboo hung with good luck symbols such as old coins (*koban*), rice sacks, and bream. Like waves, visitors surge to buy them.

**(Right) Osaka Castle**   Osaka Castle was completed in 1585, having been conceived by Toyotomi Hideyoshi as a structure worthy of one who had brought the greater part of Japan under his sway, and built by the coopted efforts of *daimyo* (feudal lords) from around the country.   What makes the castle distinctive is its massive stone walls, some blocks of which measure sixty square meters in area.   Some stone blocks display the crests and marks of the *daimyo* who donated them and who supervised the building.

After Hideyoshi's death, Tokugawa Ieyasu, who inherited his power, captured and burned the castle in a conflict over the succession. Though it was rebuilt a short while later, it was again destroyed, this time by lightning.   The present structure, the main keep only, is a reconstruction dating from 1931, modeled on pictures depicting it during Hideyoshi's time. This allows us to imagine the imposing appearance of the original.   Osaka residents still call it "Hideyoshi's Castle," and look upon it with deep affection.

**(Left) Hozenji Yokocho at night**   Hozenji Yokocho is a popular pleasure district where scores of small eating and drinking places crowd together along narrow alleys (*yokocho*). Long ago, it was part of the precinct of a temple called Hozenji.   Late in the eighteenth century, itinerant playhouses and sideshows opened here, and it became a center of plebeian entertainment.   The only reminders of its religious connections are small chapels dedicated to Jizo, a popular bodhisattva connected with the salvation of children in particular, and to Kompira, a deity regarded as the protector of fishermen and sailors.   They are the foci of devotion of the common people, especially entertainers and performers, and redolent of the atmosphere of plebeian Osaka.

## Himeji Castle

**The main donjon (*tenshukaku*) of Himeji Castle**   Himeji Castle is located in the city of Himeji, Hyogo Prefecture, some ninety kilometers to the west of Osaka.   At the end of the sixteenth century it was briefly in the hands of Toyotomi Hideyoshi; a retainer, Ikeda Terumasa (1564–1613), then became its lord and undertook, over nine years (1601–1609), the massive reconstruction that has left us with the castle we know today.

Viewed laterally, the castle seems to assume the shape of a white egret stretching out its wings, and therefore is known popularly as Egret Castle.   The beauty of its surrounding white walls and its grand scale have ensured that it ranks first of Japanese castles.   The main donjon, the highest structure, is forty-five meters high, and it and its surrounding structures have been designated National Treasures.

Because, naturally, the prime function of the castle was defense, its interior is solid and simple, reflecting practicality above all else.   Externally, though, the castle exhibits an elegance inherited from the temple architectural tradition.   This aesthetic consciousness, which demands beauty in even a building intended for war, is unexpected in warriors.   Still, these were men to whom the morrow might as easily bring death as life, and they doubtless would have preferred to be dependent for their safety on a fortress that was also a thing of beauty.

# CHUGOKU

The Chugoku region covers the western part of Honshu, and is divided into two districts by a central mountainous area, San'in along the Sea of Japan to the north, and San'yo along the Inland Sea to the south. Winter in the San'in district is marked by day after day of overcast skies, and heavy rain and snow, and the district was consequently comparatively late developing. However, it has a rich historical and cultural tradition; before the political unification of Japan and the domination of the Yamato district from around the seventh century, a great kingdom existed in the Izumo area of Shimane Prefecture and vied with Yamato for power.

The San'yo district has mild winters and a low yearly rainfall. Since ancient times it has served as a corridor between Kyushu, the portal for continental culture, and the Kinki region, the center of government; and later it forged its own trading links with China and the continent. Favorable climatic conditions and good communications allowed the coastal areas to develop as an industrial region. There are nevertheless many old and historical castle towns and ports centering on Hiroshima.

## Reflected Images: Itsukushima and Kintaibashi

(**Above left**) **The** *torii* **of Itsukushima Shrine** The Itsukushima Shrine is located on Miyajima ("Shrine Island"), set in the Inland Sea in Hiroshima Prefecture. It was built at the end of the sixth century as a shrine dedicated to the sea goddess; the splendid shrine complex of today dates from the middle of the twelfth century when Taira no Kiyo-mori (1118–1181), the dominant political figure of his times, gave the shrine his lavish support. As befits a shrine to the sea goddess, the buildings jut out over the sea, so that at high tide they seem to be floating on the waves. A sixteen-meter tall red *torii*, marking the entrance, stands in the sea, and can be reached on foot at low tide. Kiyomori, though born into a warrior family, lived and governed according to the mores of the aristoc-racy, and so he is considered, not the founder of warrior rule in Japan, but the last of the aristocractic power holders. The Itsukushima Shrine combines the warrior's liking for things done on a grand scale with an aesthetic consciousness typical of the Kyoto aristocracy.

Miyajima is counted as one of the three scenic wonders of Japan with Matsushima (Tohoku) and Amano-hashidate (Kinki).

**Kintai Bridge and cherry blossoms**  The Kintai Bridge, spanning the Nishiki river at Iwakuni, Yamaguchi Prefecture, is of unique shape and construction, consisting of five arches built entirely of wood without the use of nails.  Because the previous bridges had tended to be swept away when the river flooded, the lord of the Iwakuni domain in the late seventeenth century decided to erect a new one using the latest technology available. The arches nearest the river banks are lightly curved, while the three middle arches describe a large arc.  It is this rhythm of strong and weak that gives the bridge its beauty.  Legend says that the bridge was built so that it could be destroyed to prevent an enemy attack by removing its main wedges.

Three hundred cherry trees have been planted near the bridge's approaches, and when they bloom the sight is breathtaking. We must praise the energy and the insight that raised the bridge from a practical instrument to a thing of beauty.

## The San'in Kyoto

**(Above left) The castle town of Tsuwano** Tsuwano in Shimane Prefecture is a quiet and placid castle town, one of those historical towns resembling Kyoto that the Japanese like to call "Little Kyotos." The white walls of samurai houses serenely line the streets, and we can still see today carp swimming in the water conduits along the sides of the roads.

**(Below left) The heron dance** The heron dance is held on the 20th and 27th of every July during the Gion Festival at the Tsuwano Yasaka Shrine as a ritual performed before the god. Two dancers, representing a male and a female white heron, tread slow and measured steps to the accompaniment of flutes and drums. The heron dance originated at Kyoto's Gion (Yasaka) Shrine, and came to Tsuwano via Yamaguchi. In recent years it has been reintroduced from Tsuwano to Kyoto and revived there after a long break.

**(Right) The Izumo Shrine** The Great Shrine of Izumo is sacred to Okuninushi no Mikoto, who was said to have ruled the area long ago. With the Ise Shrine it is of very old standing. According to Japanese mythology, the heavenly realm (Takamagahara) was the domain of Amaterasu Omikami, the ancestor deity of the imperial family, and the earthly realm (Japan, the Central Land of the Reed Plains) that of Okuninushi, based at Izumo. Okuninushi gave over his rule at Amaterasu's orders and built himself a great palace for his retirement, on the site of which, legend tells us, is now the Izumo Shrine. Though myth, we can conjecture from this tale that Izumo once had a power to rival Yamato's.

A cradle of Japanese mythology, the Izumo Shrine today is popular as being sacred to marriage. Young and newly-wedded couples make constant pilgrimage there. The shrine buildings, in their surroundings of verdant greenery, date from a reconstruction done in the latter half of the eighteenth century.

# SHIKOKU

Shikoku is an island spanning the Inland Sea to the south of the Chugoku region. Mountains divide the northern and southern parts. The northern side has a climate like San'yo's in the Chugoku region with low rainfall and long stretches of fine weather. Winters in the southern part are mild, summers are wet, and typhoons often sweep through.

Though Shikoku is geographically not far from Kyoto, the fact that it is an island made it seem isolated from the central region. It was consequently both a place of exile for political offenders, and a refuge for those on the losing side in wars. Development came late, so that much of the island remains wild and untamed. It is now facing a new phase in its progress with the completion of the Great Seto Bridge in 1988, linking it directly by rail and road to Honshu.

## Stone Steps and a Vine Bridge

(Right) **The stone steps leading up to the Kotohira Shrine** The Kotohira Shrine in Kagawa Prefecture has been revered from ancient times as a protector of sailors and fishermen. The cult was spread by merchants from the Inland Sea area throughout Japan especially in and after the eighteenth century, and the shrine attracted large numbers of common people on pilgrimage. It was a "boom" period for travel by ordinary people; large numbers toured the shrines of Kyoto, visited the Ise Shrine, and came to Kotohira, the three popular destinations.

There are 785 steps leading from the shrine entrance to the main sanctuary, and a further 583 from there to the inner sanctuary. With such an effort required, many people would hire a palanquin to ascend, this being the most used vehicle until Japan opened its doors to the West 130 years ago.

(Following page) **The Suspension Bridge at Iya** A suspension bridge woven from wild vines is still to be seen spanning the Iya river in the southwest of Tokushima Prefecture. It was to the mountainous and largely unexplored Iya region that survivors of the defeated Heike (Taira clan) are reputed to have fled at the end of the twelfth century when Minamoto no Yoritomo emerged victorious from the civil war. They are said to have made their bridges of wild creepers so that if they were attacked by the enemy they could quickly cut them down. Whatever the reason behind their making, the bridges were a testimonial to the strength of the common people. Today only one remains, designated an Important Cultural Property, as a reminder of the practical wisdom of people living in a mountainous region.

# KYUSHU

The Kyushu region, forming the southwestern extremity of Japan, is made up of the third largest island in the country (Kyushu) and the Nansei Islands stretching like pebbles from Kyushu south to Taiwan. The proximity of the region to the Korean Peninsula and the Asian continent ensured that it played an early and prominent role in the introduction of continental culture to Japan. Between two thousand and fifteen hundred years ago, Kyushu was the most culturally advanced region in Japan.

The central part of Kyushu is covered by rugged mountains, from which plains stretch to the north. It was northern Kyushu that was long the gateway for continental culture, and it remains today the fourth largest economic and industrial area in Japan, centering on the cities of Fukuoka and Kita Kyushu, which have more than a million inhabitants. Southern Kyushu is hilly; here cows and horses are raised and vegetables grown.

Okinawa, to the south, is the chief of the Nansei Islands, and here a distinctive island history and culture remain. Okinawa Prefecture consists of a chain of islands making up the westernmost part of Japan. It is a subtropical area where the sun shines the year around. Long ago it had close relations with China, but it came under Japanese influence from the seventeenth century on, and was formally made a part of Japan in 1879. More than 100,000 people here lost their lives in 1945 during the final stages of the Pacific War. Placed under American control after the war, it was returned to Japan in 1972.

## Buddhist Rock Sculptures

(**Left**) **The stone Buddhas of Usuki** Oita Prefecture in the northeastern part of Kyushu is famous for the many stone Buddhas that were carved between seven and twelve hundred years ago. After it had been introduced from Korea, Buddhism gave rise in the Kinki region to impressive temples and orthodox sculpture. In Kyushu, however, Buddhism merged with local beliefs, and in the mountains many centers for ascetic training and sacred sites came into existence. The sandstone formed by volcanic ash from Mount Aso was particularly suitable for carving Buddhist statues, and especially popular were large carvings (*magaibutsu*) made in cliff sides. There are more than sixty such Buddhist figures, large and small, in the Usuki district. The photograph shows a cliff sculpture from which the head has fallen away and now lies on the valley floor. Nevertheless, we can see how skillfully it was carved, with its full cheeks and half-closed eyes, in no way inferior to the more usual statues of wood or metal.

**(Above) The cliff Buddhas of Fukoji**  More Buddhist cliff sculptures are to be found in the Asaji district in the southwestern part of Oita Prefecture, overlooking a river that flows through the precinct of the temple Fukoji. Characteristic of the group is a statue of Fudo Myoo (Acala), with attendants standing to either side, thought to have been made about seven hundred years ago.  Standing 8.3 meters high, it is the tallest of Oita's Buddhist rock sculptures.

There are also Buddhist rock carvings on the Kunisaki Peninsula in northeastern Kyushu, an area known as a treasure house of Kyushu Buddhist culture.

## Homeland of the Imperial Ancestors

(**Above left**) **Takachihonomine** The mountain Takachihonomine, whose peak is 1,574 meters above sea level, is in Miyazaki Prefecture, in Kyushu's southeast. Legend says that it was to this mountain that Ninigi no Mikoto, the grandson of Amaterasu, descended from Takamagahara (the High Celestial Plain) when given control over the Central Land of the Reed Plains (Japan). The legendary first emperor of Japan, Jimmu, great-grandson of Ninigi no Mikoto, grew up in the Takachiho palace, before leading an army from Kyushu to the Kinki region, where he set up a new government. This legend would make Takachihonomine the birthplace of Japan's imperial line.

The mountain is one of the main peaks of the Kirishima Volcanic Zone, and clothed in much mystery.

**(Above right) The *kagura* of Takachiho district** *Kagura* (sacred dances) of the Takachiho region center on themes from Japanese mythology, for it was here that legend said that the progenitor of the imperial line descended from heaven. The "Night Kagura" seen here illustrates the following legend. Amaterasu, the Sun Goddess, angered at her brother Susanoo's boisterous and unruly behavior, hides herself in the Heavenly Rock Cave (Ama no Iwaya), plunging the world into darkness. The gods in consternation wonder what to do, and have the goddess Uzume perform a comical dance. Curious about the laughter she hears, Amaterasu peeps outside, and as she does so Tajikarao, a god famed for his strength, forces the rock open. Light is restored to the world.

This *kagura*, which lasts more than twenty hours, is performed into the night in various villages of the district between November and the beginning of February. During this time, wherever you go you will hear the music of *kagura* in one village or another. It is a tranquil scene, reminiscent of the mythological age. Nowadays, the *kagura* is performed every day at the Takachiho Shrine regardless of season for visiting tourists.

## The Traditions of the South

(**Above right**) **Women in Okinawan costume in front of Shurei no mon**   The Shurei no mon, erected around the sixteenth century, is one of the eight gates of Shuri Castle, where the Okinawan kings used to live.   The original, a National Treasure, was destroyed during the Pacific War; the present reconstruction dates from 1958.   The gate is a symbol of Okinawa, whose historical remains were all lost in the war.

(**Below**) **The Izaiho ritual**   The Izaiho ritual is performed every twelve years at Kudakajima in Chinen, Okinawa.   Kudakajima has long been revered as a sacred island.   All women who are born or who marry here have to become priestesses of the gods (*noro*), and the ceremony of their initiation is called *izaiho*. All women on the island between 30 and 70 perform the ritual, and men also take part.   It is a particularly important ceremony for women between 30 and 41, who are attending for the first time, for during it they receive spiritual power from their ancestors and gain the qualifications they need for becoming *noro*. The festival maintains the traditions of the ancient society, where men held authority over government, and women over religion, supporting them.

# AESTHETICS IN DAILY LIFE

## The Tokonoma

●**The symbol of a Japanese room** One of the most distinctive features of the traditional Japanese room is the *tokonoma*, or alcove. The *tokonoma* is a raised section of floor set within a wall, in which is hung pictorial or calligraphic scrolls, and ornaments and flowers displayed.

Not all Japanese-style rooms have a *tokonoma*, for it is considered a space special to the rooms where guests are received. People from overseas tend to find it strange that when such visitors are seated in the place of honor, their backs are to the *tokonoma*, from which position they are unable to see the scroll hung there. The reason for the custom can be found in the historical development of the *tokonoma*.

●**A formal space** The origins of the *tokonoma* may be traced to the *jodan*, a small raised platform in a room where the master, or the chief guest in a tea ceremony, was seated. Though the early tea ceremony was strongly influenced by Chinese aesthetics, and created an atmosphere splendid rather than severe, it was transformed during the sixteenth century with the appearance of such masters as Sen no Rikyu into a simple and tranquil gathering taking place in a small tea hut constructed of the simplest materials. The dimensions of the tea room in turn became much smaller, as did those of the raised platform, and by the seventeenth century, the form of the *tokonoma* had become fixed into what we know today: a decorative space where people do not enter. The custom of the guest seated in front of the *tokonoma* clearly derives from the raised platform, *jodan*.

●**A decorative space** Even before the evolution of the *tokonoma*, rooms had a place where calligraphy and paintings could be dis-played. The wall was sunk back fifty or sixty centimeters and backed with a thick board on which paintings were hung. This feature, a stationary wall, was called the *oshiita* ("pressed board"), and came into use during the fourteenth and fifteenth centuries.

The *tokonoma* can be considered to be derived from both the elements outlined above, the formal space of the raised platform, and the decorative space of the stationary wall. It owes its subsequent development to the architecture of the tea room. The quiet, unadorned, refined spirit of the *wabi* (simple and austere) style of tea ceremony that Sen no Rikyu emphasized appealed to the disposition of the nature-loving Japanese, and the *tokonoma* that had become a decorative feature within the context of that ceremony became widely incorporated into the family home. It has continued to be central to the daily life of the Japanese as the symbol of that which is set apart, a space with artistic and spiritual meaning.

▲**Tokonoma** The hanging scroll should contain a long, narrow picture, or calligraphy.

# Shoji and Fusuma

●**Flexibility as a mark of the Japanese room** We usually think of house interiors as being partitioned by walls and doors, but the space within a Japanese dwelling is rather divided up by walls, *shoji* and *fusuma*, sliding doors made of paper or cloth on a wood lattice. Such "doors" are different in concept from the fixed door made entirely of wood.

The Western tradition of architecture considers doors to serve the function of closing off rooms that are not in use, to be opened only when people want to go in or out. *Shoji* and *fusuma*, by contrast, can be easily removed, so that connecting rooms can be easily joined to make a larger space as the wall area of Japanese rooms is small compared with that of Western houses. This gives great flexibility of use to the Japanese room. If large numbers of people are expected, the *fusuma* can be removed and the room enlarged. Since as well the Japanese have traditionally used little heavy furniture like beds or large tables, a single room can be used for sleeping or eating equally easily. There is absolutely no need to specify a room by its function.

In such flexibility in terms of practical needs, we can discern the rational approach that the Japanese have toward daily living.

●**Shoji** *Shoji* are sliding doors constructed of a wood lattice covered by a single thin sheet of paper, leaving one side of the framework exposed. In general they are used to divide rooms from inside or outside corridors. The paper construction allows natural ventilation and warmth to permeate the room while cutting off draughts and wind. The even light that filters through the paper creates a tranquil atmosphere within the room, and the *shoji's* simple design of white paper and unpainted wood makes for a bracing living environment. The shadowy patterns of leaves and light that dance on the *shoji* are beloved of the Japanese, and feature as a theme in songs and novels.

●**Fusuma** *Fusuma* are room dividers, made of thick paper stretched over both sides of a wooden framework. Removed, they create a larger space, and in place they make independent rooms. They are decorated with paintings of natural scenery, or of flowers and birds; the nature of the painting is decisive in giving a room its distinctive atmosphere and impression.

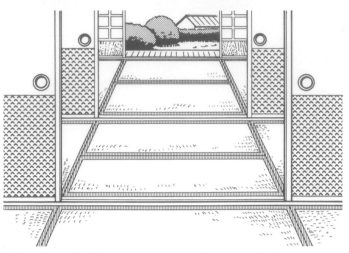

▲**Interior of a Japanese room** A room divided by fusuma can be enlarged by opening or removing them.

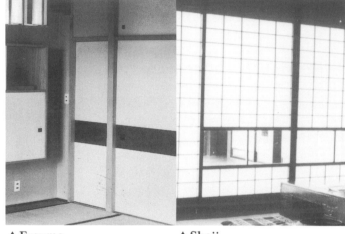

▲**Fusuma**　　　　　▲**Shoji**

●**Types of shoji**

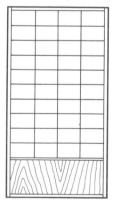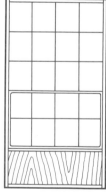

●**Types of fusuma**

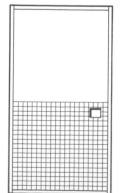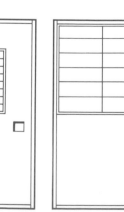

# The Garden and the Outer Corridors

●**Gardens for viewing** The Japanese love gardens. Even the smallest space is filled with trees and plants.

Japanese gardens are of a different nature from European ones. The Western tradition regards a garden as a place for recreation, where people, for instance, can sit and enjoy the sun's warmth. In certain cases, some estates can be so large that their owners can even hunt in them. The Japanese garden is considered rather a place to bring ease of mind to the viewer, sitting inside a room or in the outer corridor. Of course in Japan, too, there is a tradition of a strolling garden, but even here, spiritual tranquility rather than recreation is the object.

●**The garden as a separate world** In contemplating their gardens, the Japanese do not simply look at natural beauty. Even in those gardens which have no ponds or running water, rocks and plants are used to create the effect of the sea somewhere. Thus, the Japanese as a whole tend to imagine when looking at gardens a Buddhist paradise far across the sea, or the universe contained within the small space of the garden.

●**A connecting space** Traditional Japanese houses have a long and narrow wooden corridor stretching around their interior portion, looking out onto the garden. This is called the *engawa*. There are two types, that which divides the interior of the house from the exterior and has glass *shoji*, and that which is like a passage inside the house.

While the *engawa* cannot be considered entirely interior space, nor can it be thought of as exterior space either. Rather, it is a connecting space. Old people can sit here, basking in the sun's warmth, and feel as if they were in the garden itself.

In their creation of an undefined space capable of being used according to conditions, the Japanese again reveal their flexible spirit.

●*Engawa*

●**Various types of fences** Fences are used as a simple way to enclose the grounds of a house, or to divide parts of the garden. They tend to be made of wood or bamboo in order to harmonize with the beauty of the garden. A strong protective wall, on the other hand is made of wood, mud or stone.

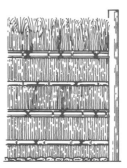
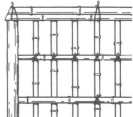
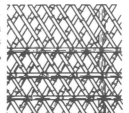

●**Typical garden styles**

▲**The Paradise garden (*jodo teien*),** constructed by the nobility between the tenth and twelfth centuries. It is characterized by a large central pond and the incorporation of natural features. The garden of Joruriji, Kyoto.

▲**The Zen garden,** the type of garden constructed within Zen temples in the fourteenth and fifteenth centuries. Typical is the rock garden, where rocks placed on white sand represent islands. Here monks underwent their spiritual training, carrying on a dialogue with the stones. The rock garden of Daisen'in, Kyoto.

▲**The Daimyo garden,** spanning the seventeenth to the nineteenth centuries, was constructed for the artistic pleasure of the feudal lords. They were large and designed for strolling, allowing seasonal changes to be savored. Ritsurin Park, Takamatsu, Kagawa Prefecture.

# A Culture of Wood, Bamboo and Paper

●**Wood** The Japanese prefer plain, unpainted wooden surfaces. From ancient times they have believed that trees themselves contain a spirit, or that trees are the vessels into which *kami* (deities) can be summoned. Even after a tree has been cut down, a certain spiritual attachment to it continues, and plain, unpainted wood has been valued for its purity and sacredness.

Plain wood is used in Japanese houses to take full advantage of its natural beauty in such features as exposed pillars and the framework of *shoji*. Cutting boards in the kitchen likewise are made of it, as are chopsticks.

●**Bamboo** The Japanese as a race love bamboo, being attracted by its remarkable vitality and fertility and its mysterious hollowness. The beauty of its straight and upright stance makes it an appealing symbol of a character, forthright and honest, pure and resolute, strong in body and mind.

Bamboo is used extensively for fences, for the decorative pillar of the *tokonoma*, for water pipes in gardens, for blinds, and for everyday articles such as baskets, plates and chopsticks. It is particularly appreciated by practitioners of the tea ceremony for its delicacy and lightness, and is widely employed in the architecture of the tea room and in tea ceremony utensils and implements.

●**Paper** Japanese paper (*washi*) is both beautiful and strong, characteristics which allow it to be used in a variety of ways in everyday life. It is employed to the greatest effect in traditional houses in *shoji* and *fusuma*. The soft light reflected through the thin paper of the *shoji* gives a room a certain softness and tranquility. *Shoji* also function as a natural temperature and humidity control, regulating the entry of air from without into the room.

White paper is the symbol of purity, and represents a mind of faith. Even now, white paper is used in Shinto rituals in the form of *gohei* (purificatory paper strips), *tamagushi* (oracle slips), and *shimenawa* (sacred straw ropes). It is employed in the calligraphy and paintings adorning the *tokonoma*, in paper dolls, and in decorative lanterns.

●**Articles made of wood**

▶**tansu,** cupboards for clothing and decorative articles.

▼**manaita,** cutting boards for fish and vegetables.

▲**oke,** pails used for washing rice and vegetables.

▲**wooden boxes,** containers for small articles.

▲**oke,** tubs used for sushi and fish.

●**Articles made of bamboo**

▲**bamboo baskets,** used for carrying things.

▲**kori,** used for storing clothing.

◀**flower vases,** the central stem is filled with water.

●**Articles made of paper**

▲**uchiwa,** a flat fan.

▲**paper dolls,** made with *washi*, the distinctive Japanese paper.

▲**the Japanese umbrella,** its spines made of bamboo and covered with oiled paper.

▲**shimenawa,** long, thin strips of white paper marking that a place is considered sacred.

# Tableware

●**Concern for tableware** Mealtimes are, of course, primarily for satisfying hunger; the Japanese though have tended to take them further, regarding them also as an expression of culture. They attach importance not only to the taste of the food, but also to the dishes in which it is served and how it is arranged in those dishes, for these must be in harmony with the food itself. There is as much concern for the tableware as for the cooking, and the Japanese say that a first-rate cook must always be thinking of the presentation as much as the taste when he or she prepares a meal.

The wide variety of tableware to be found in Japan is divided according to use and season. Dishes have to match the food in terms of shape, color and size. Multi-purpose plates such as are to be found in Western cooking are not used.

●**A variety of utensils** Tableware differs according to the food being served.

●**The use of empty space** Ample room must be left in dishes after the food has been served. Even a small amount of food may be displayed in a large dish, with a lot of surface space left unoccupied. It is not the custom in Japan to fill a dish to its limit—even a teacup is filled to only seventy percent of its capacity, allowing the remaining space to fulfill a function like that of a lingering note. Other types of food will be displayed at an even lower ratio than that. This is an expression of the feeling that the Japanese have for empty space, a balance between what is and what is not that is symbolized also in the Noh play and in haiku, and in the importance given to undecorated space in traditional painting. How much food is placed in a dish, and where it is placed, express an aesthetic and spiritual dimension of consciousness. There is true richness in being able to "taste" the seasons as well as the mind of the person who made the food.

①**Meshiwan, Chawan (Ricebowl)** Rice is the main food of the Japanese. It is usual for each member of the family to have his or her own rice bowl, with its distinctive pattern and color. Usually people have two or three bowls of rice during a meal. A slightly larger bowl may be used to ensure the rice does not get cold. When only one serving of rice is to be given, a bowl called a *domburi* is used.

②**Sara** Flat, shallow plates are used to serve side dishes, and are probably the most widely used of all tableware. Of varying designs and shapes, they are brought out according to the season. For example, there is a sense of incongruity in using a plate shaped like an autumn leaf in spring.

③**Hachi** Dishes (*hachi*) are deeper than plates (*sara*), and are used when serving side dishes such as chilled *tofu* (bean curd) and salad.

④**Wan (Bowl)** While most tableware is made of pottery, lacquered wooden bowls are used for serving soups, clear or miso based. Being wooden, they can be handled even when full of hot soup. Since soups are drunk directly from the bowl, the wooden surface also makes for a pleasant texture when the lips meet the rim.

⑤**Chawan** Of the many sizes and shapes of tableware, perhaps the most refined is the bowl used during

the tea ceremony. Until the middle of the sixteenth century, tableware, whether deep or shallow, were generally round; it was Sen no Rikyu, the great tea master, who brought a change to this tradition. He was drawn to the comparatively unrefined, handmade style of beauty then dominant on the Korean Peninsula, and had tea bowls made for himself incorporating that aesthetic. Furuta Oribe (1544–1615), his disciple and successor, took this trend even further, attempting to achieve an unfettered freedom of design. The Japanese, as a race preferring asymmetry to symmetry, here threw off the Chinese influence which had been dominant until then and began to produce a pottery that corresponded to their own aesthetic consciousness.

⑥**Tokkuri** The sake jar (*tokkuri, ochoshi*) is used for heating sake, by placing it in hot water. Originally large jars did exist, but it is now usual for them to be of a capacity of 180 cc, given the popularity of the custom of heating sake. The sake is poured from the jar into a small cup.

⑦**Choko** Small sake cups are called *choko* or *choku*, and larger ones *guinomi*. They come in a large number of designs. Like the chawan, they come directly into contact with the lips, and so smoothness is of great importance. Such sensitivity toward the sense of touch is a special feature of Japanese culture.

# The Kimono

●**Beauty in color**  Today, the kimono is no longer worn as everyday dress.  All the same, the Japanese are deeply attached to it, and many women in particular will wear it for ceremonial occasions and special functions. The kimono's beauty is revealed in its coloring and patterns.  Favorite designs are based on abstractions of familiar plants and birds. Here again we see the Japanese liking for living at one with nature.

Young women wear colorful patterns, but for everyday wear colors are more subdued, grays, browns and dark blues in subtle gradations, giving rise to a culture based upon middle tones.  There are no rules concerning the color of kimonos, though the Japanese do tend to think of white as standing for purity and the sacred, of red as symbolizing vitality, able to repel evil spirits, and of purple as signifying nobility.

The kimono is worn with a little of the lining, in a contrasting color, showing at the hem, and with the white collar of the long undergarment exposed at the neckline.  Showing off the beauty of the kimono necessitates much attention to detail.

●**Beauty of shape**  Perhaps it is the sash (*obi*) that best enables the kimono's beauty of shape to be appreciated.  Not only does the design of the *obi* enhance the front of the kimono, but the way it is tied behind emphasizes the beauty of the back as well.  The *obi* originally was no more than seven or eight centimeters wide, and it could be tied at either front or back in any way at all.  Its width broadened gradually, and it became the fixed custom to tie it in a wide fold at the back.

The kimono's beauty is further brought out by how hair ornaments, footwear and other accessories match it.

▲**Male Japanese dress**
Above, a crested kimono; below, *hakama*, resembling a pleated skirt.

▲**Female Japanese dress**
The kimono worn when visiting.

●**Children wearing kimono**

▶**Children's festival dress**  Children usually wear kimono when observing auspicious events. The photograph shows children on the occasion of Shichi-go-san, held every year on November 15 among girls of seven, boys of five, and boys and girls of three to celebrate their growth.

●**Traditional Japanese footwear**

To the left of the photograph is men's footwear, to the right, women's. At the bottom are *geta*, wooden clogs with two supports, and *zori*, flat sandals made of a soft material like straw.

●**Obi**

The obi is a long, broad sash wrapped around the waist, securing the kimono. Three to four meters long, it is tied very tightly in a decorative tie at the back of the body: it is therefore difficult for one person to manage alone.

# Patterns and Designs

●**Designs taken from nature** Traditionally, kimono, utensils, cosmetic articles, toilet cases, and other small items were decorated with various patterns, generally those taking nature as their theme such as cherry blossoms in spring, running water in summer, red leaves in autumn, and snow in winter. Such patterns have grown out of the deep love for and contemplation of nature. The following lists the main categories.

•Plants—plum, cherry, pine, bamboo. The autumnal grasses pattern of pampas grass and gentians is particularly evocative of the Japanese sensibility.

•Animals—Crane, tortoise. Deer in an abstract landscape tend to typify autumn.

•Water—running water, waves, hills and streams, flowers at the water's edge, waves and seabirds. A particular feature of Japanese water patterns is the diversity of design vividly portraying the curved lines of flowing water.

•The sky—the moon, the sun, the stars, clouds.

•Objects—Implements, vehicles, court ox-cart, arrow feathers, top, folding fan. These generally are used in conjunction with a design of natural scenery.

●**Family crests** Traditionally, Japanese families and clans have had distinctive crests. On formal occasions it is the custom to wear *montsuki* traditional dress embroidered with the crest.

Crests, which had come into general use by the eleventh century, had their origin in the emblems the court nobility attached to their ox-carts to distinguish them from those of others, and in the banners warriors carried into battle. Old families take particular pride in their crests.

Most commonly used for crests are abstract designs based upon natural objects such as plants and birds.

●Plant designs

▲ Autumn grasses

▲ Pine

▲ Bamboo

▶ Plum (*Ume*)

▲ Wild cherry blossom

●Animal designs

▲ Tortoise

▼ Rabbit and waves

▼ Crane and pine trees

▼ Deer

●Water designs

▲ Breaking waves

▲ River and autumn leaves

▲ Waves and birds

▶ Abstract pattern based on waves

●Objects

▲ Arrows

▲ Fans

▲ Tops

▶ Carts in water

●Family crests

●Sky designs

▲ Lightning

▼ Breaking waves and sunrise

▲ Moon and a star

▲ Clouds

# Japanese Houses and Inns

● **Traditional life mirrored in a Japanese inn** Today foreign people visiting Japan are finding it very difficult to experience life in a traditional home. The wave of modernization and urbanization has taken away much of the old and left behind an architecture which is very much European and American in inspiration.

However, it is not impossible to experience life in a traditional Japanese house. If you travel to a hot spring resort or tourist center, you can stay in a Japanese inn (*ryokan*). A pebbled path bordered by shrubbery leads from the front gate to the entrance porch. The room to which you are shown is covered in *tatami* matting. In the center of the room is a large low table with flat cushions around it to sit on. A *tokonoma* is set into one wall, and is decorated with a hanging scroll and a flower arrangement. You gain respite from your journey sipping tea in front of the *tokonoma*.

● **The inn as an integral part of travel** Western hotels are considered primarily places to rest and sleep. By contrast, the Japanese inn itself is an important element of the journey as a whole. In a room looking out onto a quiet garden, the traveler is served a fine meal, after which he or she relaxes in a bath or hot spring. For a Japanese, the inn itself becomes the purpose of travel. There are many, particularly elderly people, for whom enjoying a stay at an inn is the ultimate pleasure.

Observing a Japanese inn built in the traditional style enables a person to appreciate the Japanese aesthetic consciousness and feeling. It is the best school for studying Japan and the Japanese.

▲ The ryokan entrance

▲ The front hall of a ryokan

▲ A guest room in a ryokan

● **Decoration in a ryokan**

Decorative pillars which maintain the natural shape of the wood. Small flowers displayed at places along the corridors soothe the weary traveler. The ability to exhibit something seemingly casually in places where the eye would not normally go is a feature of the Japanese aesthetic consciousness.

# How Inns Receive Guests

●**Personal attention** The greatest contrast between a Western-style hotel and a Japanese inn is in the personal attention given the guest. On arrival, you are welcomed politely by the proprietor and the employees, and on departure, sent off with a similarly warm farewell.

An employee guides you to your room, which, rather than being coldly numbered, is called by some name such as "Bush Clover" or "Pavilion of the Wind and the Moon," which usually has a reference to nature. Here we have again the Japanese concern with natural things.

When you go into your room, you will be brought tea, light cakes or crackers, and a wet towel to wipe your hands. This towel, called an *oshibori*, which will be cold in summer and warm in winter, is also used in ordinary homes when serving tea or a meal to a guest. It conveys to the guest a sense of refreshment and warm welcome, and as such is an example of the informal but caring attitude to be found in the traditional culture of the Japanese.

●**A world apart** The best thing about a Japanese inn is the sense of having arrived in another, more leisurely world, released from the pressures of everyday life. All the guests change into the same light kimono (*yukata*), in which they are free to wander around the inn itself or the streets outside. On the surface then there is no difference between high and low. There are no demands for a formal appearance at meals. Everyone is bathed in a feeling of freedom and release.

●**Individual service** A major feature of the Japanese inn is its individual service. In one sense, that is its total meaning. There are attendants for every room, who do everything that needs doing down to the tiniest detail. With the exception of those who are traveling in large groups, guests are served meals individually in their rooms. The attendants also unroll, and put away, the bedding (*futon*). Everything the traveler needs—*yukata*, hand towels, even a toothbrush—is provided by the inn.

There is no system of tipping. A gratuity might be given, but this would occur once only, not whenever a service was being done.

▲The inn keeper and his employees come out to the entrance hall to meet and greet the guest.

▲One assistant takes the guest's luggage and shows him his room.

▲As soon as the guest enters his room, he finds tea and a simple sweet awaiting him.

▲The room attendant brings the guest's meals to his room, and clears away afterwards.

▲A Japanese meal laid out. Care and delicacy can be seen in the choice of utensils.

▲Though rooms have private baths, there is also a large bath which can take up to ten people.

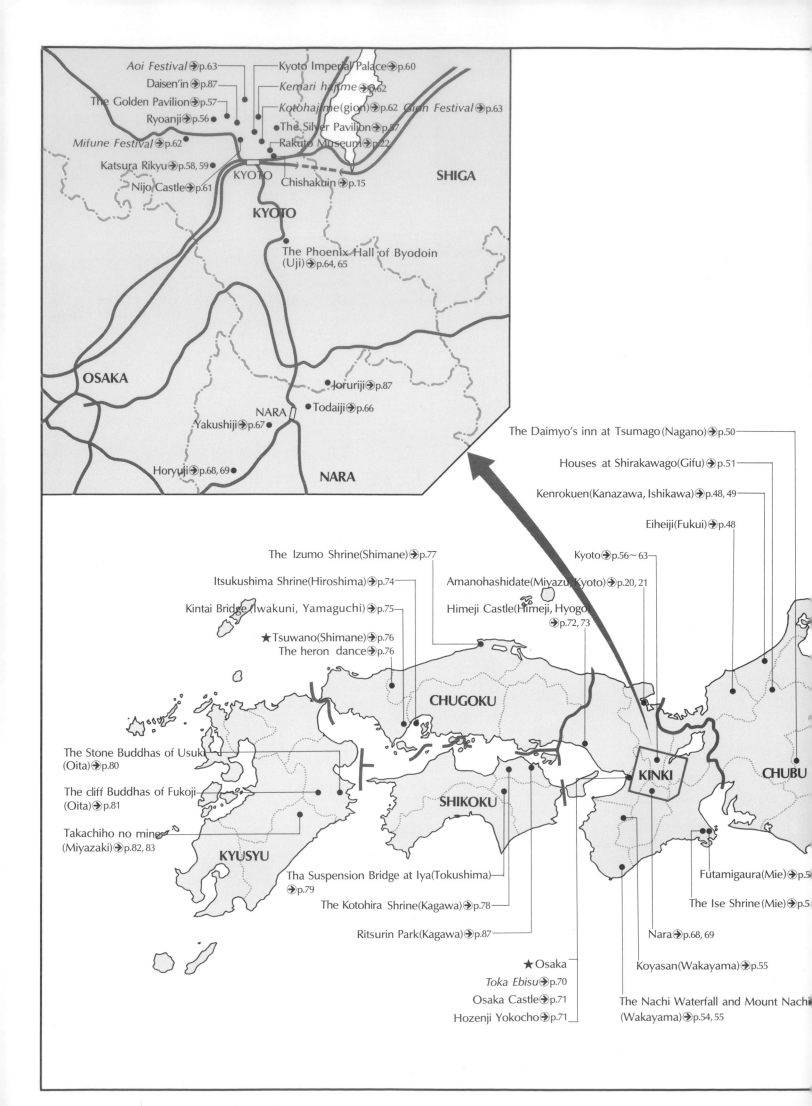

*Aoi Festival* ➜p.63
Daisen'in ➜p.87
The Golden Pavilion ➜p.57
Ryoanji ➜p.56
*Mifune Festival* ➜p.62
Katsura Rikyu ➜p.58, 59
Nijo Castle ➜p.61

Kyoto Imperial Palace ➜p.60
*Kemari hajime* ➜p.62
*Kotohajime(gion)* ➜p.62  *Gion Festival* ➜p.63
The Silver Pavilion ➜p.57
Rakuto Museum ➜p.22
Chishakuin ➜p.15

KYOTO

KYOTO

SHIGA

The Phoenix Hall of Byodoin
(Uji) ➜p.64, 65

OSAKA

Joruriji ➜p.87
Todaiji ➜p.66

NARA

Yakushiji ➜p.67

Horyuji ➜p.68, 69

NARA

The Daimyo's inn at Tsumago (Nagano) ➜p.50

Houses at Shirakawago(Gifu) ➜p.51

Kenrokuen(Kanazawa, Ishikawa) ➜p.48, 49

Eiheiji(Fukui) ➜p.48

Kyoto ➜p.56～63

The Izumo Shrine(Shimane) ➜p.77

Itsukushima Shrine(Hiroshima) ➜p.74

Amanohashidate(Miyazu, Kyoto) ➜p.20, 21

Kintai Bridge (Iwakuni, Yamaguchi) ➜p.75

Himeji Castle(Himeji, Hyogo)
➜p.72, 73

★Tsuwano(Shimane) ➜p.76
The heron dance ➜p.76

CHUGOKU

KINKI

CHUBU

The Stone Buddhas of Usuki
(Oita) ➜p.80

The cliff Buddhas of Fukoji
(Oita) ➜p.81

SHIKOKU

Takachiho no mine
(Miyazaki) ➜p.82, 83

KYUSYU

Futamigaura(Mie) ➜p.5

Tha Suspension Bridge at Iya(Tokushima)
➜p.79

The Kotohira Shrine(Kagawa) ➜p.78

Ritsurin Park(Kagawa) ➜p.87

The Ise Shrine (Mie) ➜p.5

Nara ➜p.68, 69

Koyasan(Wakayama) ➜p.55

★Osaka
*Toka Ebisu* ➜p.70
Osaka Castle ➜p.71
Hozenji Yokocho ➜p.71

The Nachi Waterfall and Mount Nachi
(Wakayama) ➜p.54, 55

# Cultural Map of Japan

- The map shows the locations of the places of interest, historic sites, museums and art galleries mentioned in the text.
- The numbers indicate the page numbers where the relevant photographs appear.
- The names of the cities and prefectures where the places of interest, historic sites, museums and art galleries are located appear in brackets.

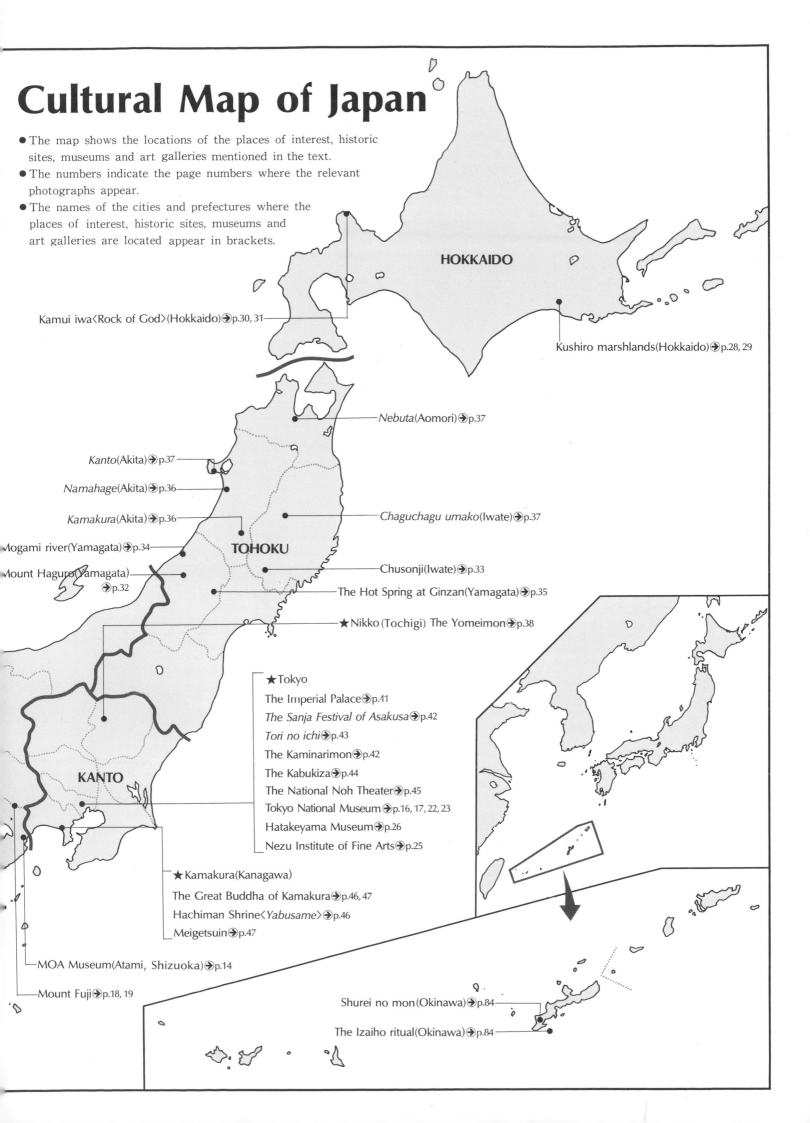

HOKKAIDO

Kamui iwa⟨Rock of God⟩(Hokkaido)➔p.30, 31

Kushiro marshlands(Hokkaido)➔p.28, 29

*Nebuta*(Aomori)➔p.37

*Kanto*(Akita)➔p.37

*Namahage*(Akita)➔p.36

*Kamakura*(Akita)➔p.36

*Chaguchagu umako*(Iwate)➔p.37

Mogami river(Yamagata)➔p.34

TOHOKU

Mount Haguro(Yamagata)➔p.32

Chusonji(Iwate)➔p.33

The Hot Spring at Ginzan(Yamagata)➔p.35

★ Nikko (Tochigi) The Yomeimon➔p.38

★Tokyo
The Imperial Palace➔p.41
*The Sanja Festival of Asakusa*➔p.42
*Tori no ichi*➔p.43
The Kaminarimon➔p.42
The Kabukiza➔p.44
The National Noh Theater➔p.45
Tokyo National Museum➔p.16, 17, 22, 23
Hatakeyama Museum➔p.26
Nezu Institute of Fine Arts➔p.25

KANTO

★Kamakura(Kanagawa)
The Great Buddha of Kamakura➔p.46, 47
Hachiman Shrine⟨*Yabusame*⟩➔p.46
Meigetsuin➔p.47

MOA Museum(Atami, Shizuoka)➔p.14

Mount Fuji➔p.18, 19

Shurei no mon(Okinawa)➔p.84

The Izaiho ritual(Okinawa)➔p.84

CREDITS
*We are grateful to the following for cooperation and permission to reproduce the photographs:*

Asukaen, BON COLOR LAB., Byodoin, Chishakuin, Chusonji, Daisen'in, Gakken Photo Library, Ginkakuji, Ginzan Hot Spa Tourist Office, Hatakeyama Museum, Hidesaburo Hagiwara, Hiroshi Hamakawa, Horyuji, Ise Shrine, Izumo Shrine, Joruriji, Katsuichi Goto, Kinkakuji, Kyoto National Museum, Kyoto Office of the Imperial Household, Meigetsuin, MOA Museum of Art, National Noh Theater, National Theater, Nezu Institute of Fine Arts, Nijo Castle, Rakuto Museum, Ryoanji, Ryu Shinohara, Sankeien, Seikado, Shigeo Okamoto, Tadao Kodaira, TAKING, TANKEI, Todaiji, Tokugawa Art Museum, Tokyo National Museum, Toshogu, Zagyoso Inn, others.